EAT, DRINK, AND BE green

PRAISE FOR *EAT, DRINK, AND BE GREEN*

"Michele Nielson has done an outstanding job developing recipes for those looking to live a healthier lifestyle. Not only do the recipes taste great, her thorough explanation of the ingredients makes understanding each recipe clear and simple."

—CHEF TOM WOODBURY, author of *Eat Fresh: Quick and Easy Meals* and TV personality

"The living, fresh, green energy of green smoothies and raw foods deeply nourishes our hungry cells and can help us become healthier and more connected to our own nature—inside and outside. Enjoy Michele's wonderful recipes and throw 'green parties' for your friends and family. Bring green into every day and begin the journey of true nourishment!"

—ANDREA NOSSEM, author of *Grüne Smoothies* and *Green Detox*

EAT, DRINK, AND BE *green*

easy and delicious recipes for a healthy lifestyle

MICHELE NIELSON

FRONT TABLE BOOKS | AN IMPRINT OF CEDAR FORT, INC. | SPRINGVILLE, UTAH

To my parents who taught me to be passionate about fresh fruits and vegetables, and to my husband who embarked on this smoothie adventure with me and who remains my favorite "guinea pig."

ISBN 13: 978-1-4621-1614-0

Published by Front Table Books, an imprint of Cedar Fort, Inc.
2373 W. 700 S., Springville, UT 84663
Distributed by Cedar Fort, Inc., www.cedarfort.com

Library of Congress Control Number: 2014959235

Cover design by Lauren Error
Page design by M. Shaun McMurdie and Rebecca J. Greenwood
Cover design © 2015 by Lyle Mortimer
Edited by Melissa J. Caldwell

Printed in China

10 9 8 7 6 5 4 3 2 1

Contents

Introduction

THE DILEMMA

WE KNEW WE SHOULD EAT MORE VEGETABLES AND GREENS, BUT IT ALWAYS SEEMED LIKE THERE WERE SO MANY OTHER YUMMIER THINGS TO EAT!

My husband and I always tried to get the recommended five servings of fruits and vegetables a day. We ate fruit for breakfast, some kind of veggie or fruit for lunch, and a vegetable for dinner. Still it seemed like we couldn't reach five servings a day. As a cook and a foodie I was on the lookout for easy and tasty ways to get more vegetables into our diet. One day a friend recommended a book about green smoothies. Actually, the book was about what I call "intensely" green smoothies—smoothies that have at least as many greens by weight as fruit and no ingredients other than fruits and greens. I read the book and was convinced that the intensely green smoothie could help us make up our vegetable deficit since it would give each of us at least two servings of vegetables in one sitting.

> VICTORIA BOUTENKO *is credited with being the "mother of the green smoothie." She was trying to find ways to improve her health and her family's health through nutrition when she came upon research by Jane Goodall about the diet of chimpanzees in the wild. She writes, "In search of the perfect human diet, I decided to look for an animal genetically close to human beings. I found that chimpanzees share an estimated 99.4% of their genes with humans. At the same time, these animals possess an extremely strong natural immunity to AIDS, Hepatitis C, cancer, and other fatal human illnesses. I was thinking that if we share 99.4% the same genes, our diets are supposed to be 99.4% similar." The diet of wild chimpanzees is about 85 percent fruit and leaves. Chimps also eat small amounts of seeds (5%), insects (4%) and meat of animals they hunt (<2%).*
>
> *(Information taken from: http://www.rawfamily.com/green-smoothie and http://www.wildchimps.org/wcf/english/files/chimp4.htm.)*

THE UNEXPECTED RESULT

SURPRISINGLY, CONSUMING LOTS MORE GREENS IN THE FORM OF A SMOOTHIE MADE US CRAVE EVEN MORE GREENS! AND WE STARTED TO LOVE VEGGIES!

We had been drinking intensely green smoothies at least three to four days a week for about three months when a strange thing occurred: all vegetables and greens suddenly started tasting better to us. We were surprised to find each afternoon and evening that, in spite of the fact we had each had four ounces of spinach for breakfast (the equivalent of a very large bowl of spinach salad), we were craving more greens. I was shocked one evening when I asked my husband if he wanted frozen pizza for dinner or just a big salad and he said he would rather have a big salad!

At the same time we both stopped caring as much about meat, cheese and high-sugar foods. We were eating lots of greens and lots of vegetables and they tasted good!

HOW THIS BOOK CAME ABOUT

AS WE STARTED LOVING VEGGIES AND GREENS, WE WANTED LOTS MORE WAYS TO EAT THEM!

Since we were craving greens and vegetables, I started experimenting more and more with recipes based mostly on fresh greens, vegetables, and fruits. The salad recipes that were already standard in our house were great, but we were both foodies and enjoyed having a variety of flavors and textures at meals. Also, we wanted more options for enjoying our new-found love of healthy foods. This book is a result of several years of experimentation as I created many, many new recipes and also gathered and tweaked several vegetable-based recipes that were already family favorites.

ANDREA NOSSEM, *author of* Grüne Smoothies *says that people who start eating or drinking lots of greens report:*

- *feeling less hungry*
- *craving sugar less*
- *less desire to eat "unhealthy foods"*
- *less desire for foods that aren't high nutrient*
- *less desire to eat meat*
- *more desire for "green"*

Andrea Nossem. Grüne Smoothies. *Munich: Wilhelm Goldmann Verlag, 2014.*

WHAT THIS BOOK CAN DO FOR YOU

MY RECIPES MAKE IT EASIER FOR YOU TO START DRINKING INTENSELY GREEN SMOOTHIES AND START LOVING YOUR VEGETABLES!

The title of this book is based on the phrase "Eat, drink, and be merry" because when vegetables and fruits start tasting good, "eating green" is delicious and happy! There are so many fun vegetables and fruits to try, and lots of different ways to eat them! My recipes are designed to let the flavors and textures shine in delicious and easy-to-make ways, without doing too much to "hide" them.

The key to enjoying this kind of recipe, though, is getting enough greens into your diet to create the craving for more. The best way I know to do this is to start drinking intensely green smoothies. And, of course, in order to start doing that, the intensely green smoothies have to taste good! The first intensely green smoothie recipes I found and tried didn't taste good to me at all. In fact, they were quite awful! I was ready to sing, with Kermit the Frog, "It's not that easy being green!"

Smoothies that are green are just not something most people are used to, and I was no exception. I decided to keep trying and started to make up my own green smoothie recipes. I worked on them and kept tweaking until I had intensely green smoothies I could enjoy—and enjoy every day. I hope that you will enjoy them too: enough that it will make it easy for you to start to Eat, Drink, and Be Green!

Michele Nielson

Salt Lake City, Utah
November 2014
www.MichelesGreenSmoothies.com

Ready, Set . . . Green!

TO HELP YOU GET STARTED EATING GREEN, THIS SECTION HAS:

- my top five reasons to Eat, Drink, and Be Green now.
- what I call my Fridge List: little ways you can start to get more Green into your life before you even look at a recipe.
- a list of what equipment you need to make my recipes.

MY TOP FIVE REASONS TO START EATING AND DRINKING GREEN NOW:

1. **It's easier to start eating Green when you are healthy—don't put it off until you are sick!** Several people I know with health problems are under doctor's orders to avoid certain things because their digestive systems have problems or they are on medications that make them have to avoid certain things. If you wait till you are sick to start eating healthy, chances are it will be much more difficult.

2. **When you eat and drink green you feel more satisfied and have less desire to snack.** When I have a green smoothie for breakfast, I frequently don't even think about eating until lunch time.

3. **Green smoothies are really a convenience food.** Once you are used to making my green smoothies, they are so easy and quick! You can freeze them to use later and you can easily drink them in the car if you have to.

4. **You will probably experience unexpected health improvements!** For me, when I get enough greens I sleep much more soundly at night, my digestion is much calmer, and my skin feels softer.

5. **If you have kids, it will be much easier to teach them to eat and drink green when they are younger.** Research shows kids palates are most flexible when they first start eating solids. Green smoothies can be an easy thing for very young kids to enjoy. If you have older kids, teaching them about healthy eating and setting an example of healthy eating will help them develop healthier attitudes and habits as they get older. I love the Dr. Seuss book Green Eggs and Ham because it teaches a truth—people often have to have several chances to try something and several chances to sample something before they get to liking it.

EAT, DRINK, AND BE GREEN "FRIDGE" LIST

Even before you make your first intensely green smoothie, there are things you can do to start getting more "green" into your diet. The list below is my brainstorm list of easy ways to start eating healthier, in your day-to-day life as it is now. I think of this as a "fridge" list—the kind I would magnet to my fridge as a way of helping me remember things. If you want a copy to put on your fridge, you can print one out on my website (www.MichelesGreenSmoothies.com)—and it has lines for you to add your own green brainstorming! As you brainstorm, I think it is key to think about the greens, vegetables, and fruits you already like and enjoy and then find ways to bring more of that kind of nutritious-deliciousness into your life.

At home:

- Make a brainstorm list of fresh greens, veggies, and fruit you enjoy eating and try to eat them more often.
- Instead of dessert, eat some fresh berries or tropical fruit (something that seems a little indulgent so you feel pampered, not deprived).
- Instead of eating just yogurt, add fruit to it or seeds, like sunflower seeds or chia. Or, instead of buying

pre-sweetened yogurt, buy thick Greek yogurt and mix in your own fresh fruit purée. (Fruit has more nutrients than dairy.)

- Add more fresh cilantro or parsley to recipes where it won't hurt anything. Toss some fresh basil or arugula into a pasta salad.
- Keep apples or other fresh fruits and veggies out on your counter during the day and keep other snack foods out of sight so that when you feel munchy, it's easiest to eat something healthy.
- Try to eat some fresh greens or some fresh vegetables every time you eat a meal or snack.
- If eating bottled salsa, dice a tomato and add it in. It will improve the flavor as well as the nutritional value. Consider adding fresh chopped cilantro.
- Reduce the amount of dressing you need on a salad by squeezing on some fresh lemon or lime juice. This brightens the flavors and adds a boost of nutrients. Adding fresh ground black pepper to your salad can also decrease the amount of dressing you need.
- Put a salad or some fresh veggies out on the table while the rest of the meal is still cooking and call your family to dinner a few minutes early. Everyone is more likely to eat more salad or veggies if they are hungry and that's what's available!
- Read my vegetable list starting on page 78 and pick a new vegetable to try.

Away from home:

- At Subway, ask for triple spinach and leave off the cheese.
- At a party, eat more from the veggie tray or fruit tray (warn the host).
- At a banquet, ask for a double portion of vegetable and salad and less meat or starch.
- Visit a salad bar at a health food store and take a look at what they offer. Make yourself a salad and try some veggies you don't usually eat.

EQUIPMENT LIST

There are a few items of equipment you have to have in order to follow my recipes. Then there are the things that are "nice to have"—they help, but you don't have to go out and buy them in order to start eating and drinking green. Below are my two lists along with helpful info.

Have to have:

- **A BLENDER:** You really do have to have a blender to do the smoothies. I have tried doing them with a hand blender and with a food processor and it doesn't work—the smoothies just don't get smooth. All my smoothie recipes and some of my other recipes are easier if you have a high power blender like a Blendtec or a Vitamix, but any blender should work with the tips I give in the green smoothie section (page 11 and 27–29). For more information about the different types of blenders, see page 7.
- **A KITCHEN SCALE:** Electronic kitchen scales start at about fifteen dollars and are available at stores like Target and Walmart as well as kitchen stores and online. Why a scale? When it comes to measuring fruits and vegetables, a scale is the only way you can reliably reproduce a recipe. I recently heard two sisters discussing a zucchini muffin recipe they had both made. One sister's had come out delicious, the other's dry. What was the difference? Each had shredded and

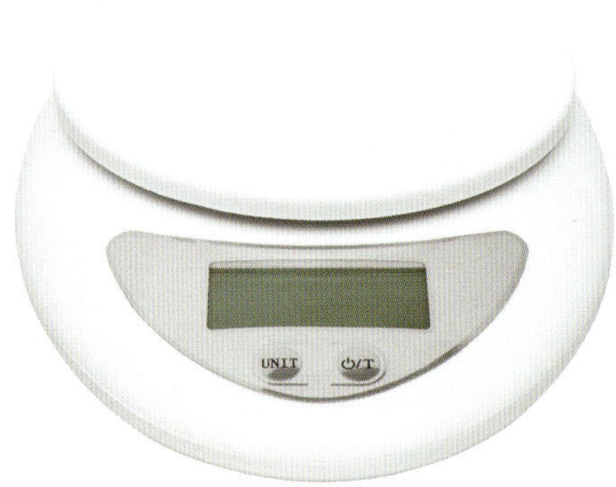

measured her zucchini in a different way. In most of my recipes I try to give a way to measure the ingredients without a scale, but almost all of them will come out better if you do use a scale. If you buy a kitchen scale and then never even use this book, I can guarantee you will still be glad you got a kitchen scale. Until you do, I suggest weighing produce at the grocery store to get the amount you need for a recipe or buying produce in preweighed packages.

- **KITCHEN SHEARS:** I use scissors during the prep of almost every meal I make. Scissors make cutting green onions or cilantro much easier. Of course you need them to open bags and packages, and they are perfect for cutting spring mix greens into smaller pieces for a more compact, easier-to-eat salad. The difference between scissors and kitchen shears is that kitchen shears come apart for easy washing. You can start out using a pair of scissors, but I recommend getting a pair of kitchen shears as soon as you can. You can find cheap ones for five to ten dollars.

- **A GOOD KNIFE:** There are lots of ways to define "a good knife." My definition of a good knife is a knife you can use to dice a fresh tomato without squishing it. If a knife can do that, it can do most other jobs too. I usually use a good serrated knife for tomatoes and cutting the peel off of oranges and other fruit and a straight edge paring knife for cutting carrots and apples. If you have a fear of knives, start by using a good serrated knife—you are less likely to injure yourself on it than on a straight knife. Keep in mind that a good sharp knife is safer than a dull one because with a dull knife you have to exert more pressure and are more likely to have a vegetable or fruit slip out from under the blade while you are cutting. For more tips on how to use knives to prepare fruits and vegetables, see page 13–14, 40 and also videos on my website: www.MichelesGreenSmoothies.com.

- **A COLANDER FOR WASHING:** I have the kind of colander that hangs over my sink, so I usually spray off my greens and then let them sit in the colander to drain while I'm preparing other things. If I am short on time or need something really dry I spread it out on

a paper towel or gently roll it in a paper towel. Because of limited time and energy, I often buy greens that are already rinsed once. When I do wash my own greens picked from the garden, I usually submerge them in water and "swish" them around a bit, then put them in the colander over my sink to drain. If you are washing lots of garden greens, it can be handy to have a salad spinner, but I generally put salad spinners in the "nice-to-have" category.

- **A SMALL COOKIE SCOOP:** Although you can get by without it, several of my recipes are much easier if you have one—enough easier that I have put this on the "must-have" list. These recipes include my Great Fruit Smoothie, Falafel with Salads, and all of my Bake-Me-Not recipes. The place I think having a scoop is most crucial is in measuring coconut oil. Coconut oil is solid at room temperature (at least in the winter) and can be

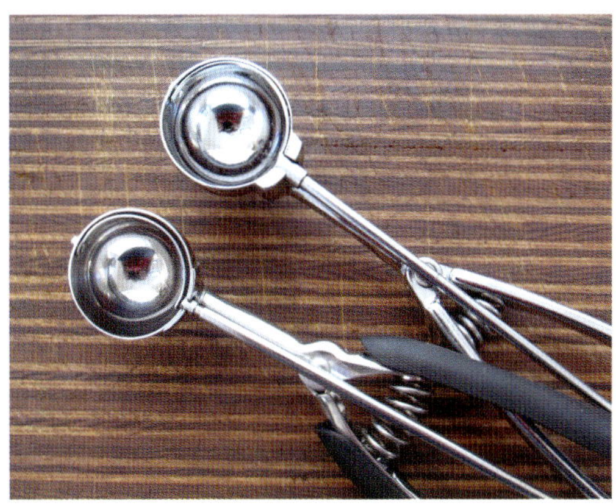

quite annoying to measure without a scoop. The size of scoop I use in my recipes is a one tablespoon scoop (same as half an ounce). It is easiest to get these online.

Nice to Have:

- **A LEMON SQUEEZER:** This is at the top of my "nice-to-have" list. These squeezers are so easy to use, I find I am no longer tempted to buy premade lemon or lime juice, and I don't dread making my own lemon or lime juice for a salad. A trick that works almost as well is to insert a fork into the center of the lemon or lime half, and squeeze the lemon or lime half around the fork while wiggling the fork—you will get much more juice out of it that way than doing it without the fork.

- **¼-CUP MEASURING PITCHER** with markings for each tablespoon like the one pictured here from Oxo. I find this to be really handy for measuring lemon, juice, lime juice, or vinegar for a salad.

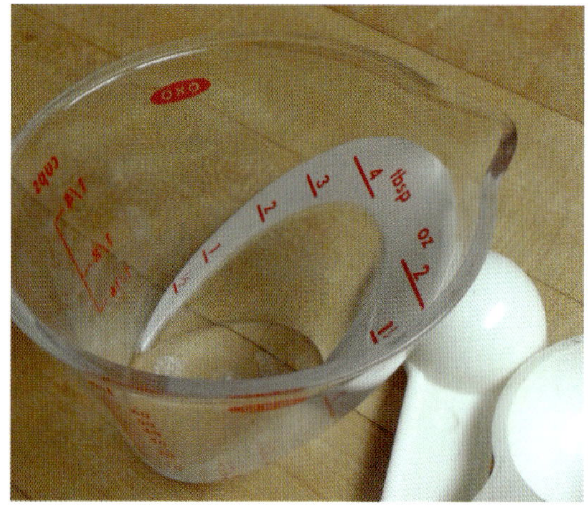

- **A SMALL OR LARGE FOOD PROCESSOR:** I try avoid doing things in my recipes that require a food processor, but sometimes there's just not a good way around it. If you only have a small one, you should still be able to make a single batch of most of my recipes.
- **AN ELECTRIC GRIDDLE:** As a cook I like an electric griddle for cooking on because it is so easy to regulate the heat. As a cookbook author, I also like electric griddles because giving instructions to cook something on the griddle at a certain temperature is so much more accurate than saying "over medium heat."
- **A SPIRALIZER:** I hadn't really even heard of a spiralizer until a few years ago, and then only in the context of making "spaghetti" out of zucchini (see page 134). I don't like having to store extra gadgets in my kitchen unless I find them really useful—and I think this one is. This was reinforced the other day when my friend and her little girl were over. I was starting to make dinner and got out the spiralizer. My friend's daughter loved turning it to make the noodles and was so interested in it that I cooked some up for her using

my Zucchini Spaghetti recipe. This three-year-old loved them and asked for more! That was all it took for my friend (who is on a tight budget) to be convinced that it was a gadget for her!

- **A GRATER OF SOME KIND:** You don't really have to have a grater, but a simple box grater or other type of simple grater can be handy when you are working with fruits and vegetables.

BLENDER NOTES:

There are two main types of blenders. I classify them as sharp-blade blenders and blunt-blade blenders. Throughout the book I refer to these blunt-blade blenders as "high-power blenders" because their blades can't and don't cut things, they just turn so fast that anything in their way gets broken down. There are some main pros and cons to each type:

Sharp-blade blenders

pros:

- they are almost universally cheaper
- they don't heat foods very much as they blend—high-speed blenders do.

cons:

- It usually takes longer to blend things—sometimes quite a lot longer.
- To get a good texture with green smoothies, you generally have to add the greens in handfuls, allowing each handful to blend before adding another.

High-power blenders

pros:

- Things get blended very quickly.
- The blunt blades make it easier to scrape everything out without your spatula getting caught or damaged.
- You can blend lots of things you can't blend in a normal blender.

cons:

- They tend to be very expensive.
- The friction generated by the blade tends to heat up the food. This can be a good thing if you are trying to get your coconut oil to emulsify with other ingredients, but it does mean that you usually have to add more ice to your smoothies.

My Evaluation:

When I started drinking green smoothies, two-hundred-plus dollars for a blender seemed like a lot. Now it feels like what I paid for my blender was a bargain because I use it so much. That being said, there is nothing at all wrong with making my recipes in a regular blender! I have a "junker" blender I got from a friend who had picked it up at a goodwill-type store. I have successfully made all but one of my blender recipes using that five-dollar blender.

If you do decide to get a high-power blender, I have a couple things for you to consider. I have used two major brands, Vitamix and Blendtec. I settled on getting a Blendtec for a couple of reasons: 1) the Vitamix had a huge on/off switch on the front of the machine. It only took accidentally hitting that switch once while the lid was off for me to learn to never take the lid off while the carafe was on the machine. Even so, I thought it would just be safer for me to get a machine with a switch in the back like it is on my Blendtec. The other main thing I liked better about the Blendtec was that the shape of the base of the carafe made it easier to scrape it out.

Designs on these machines change frequently, so these are just some things to look at as you are weighing other pros and cons.

SECTION 1

Green Smoothies

- MAKING THE INTENSELY GREEN SMOOTHIE YUMMY!
- INGREDIENTS AND TIPS
- BEFORE YOU START
- RECIPES
- FREQUENTLY ASKED QUESTIONS

MAKING THE INTENSELY GREEN SMOOTHIE YUMMY!

Several years ago I had the opportunity to spend some time in Brazil. While there, I frequently visited their juice bars. The juice bars served a huge variety of juices and smoothie-type drinks, but I was struck by the fact that despite the length of the list (up to thirty different fruit

drinks listed) almost all of the drinks on the menu contained a single fruit and very few other ingredients. It was several months after I went to Brazil that I started getting into green smoothies. I tried making some of the recipes I found in books and online. They all had long ingredient lists, which I found overwhelming. They didn't usually include exact amounts, which, as a beginner, I also found overwhelming. Worst of all, if I did gather all the ingredients and made a recipe, it still tasted terrible to me! Keep in mind that I was determined to use a formula of 50 percent greens to 50 percent fruit by weight. That is a lot of greens.

It was at that point that I started basing my smoothies on *vitaminas* (milk shakes) and *sucos* (juices) I had tried in Brazil. The first Brazilian-style green smoothie I experimented with was based on a classic Brazilian *suco*—pineapple with fresh mint. I thought the green color of the smoothie wouldn't bother me so much if I was expecting at least a hint of mint flavor and figured the mint might help mask the flavor of the greens. At the same time, I hit on the idea of putting unsweetened coconut in the smoothie and discovered that it very effectively neutralized the "green" flavor of the spinach (see page 24). The result was a delicious smoothie that my husband and I drank almost every morning for the next several months. During that time I did tests using every other fruit I could think of. Some fruits that I didn't expect to work well turned out great, while some fruits I thought would be good ended up tasting terrible (you can read more detail about this on pages 29–30).

All seven of the intensely green smoothie recipes I have included in this section are ones I find very tasty and could drink for months without feeling like I needed a change. The recipes that didn't turn out so well aren't in the book. I've kept the ingredient lists relatively simple and the measurements exact so that you can jump in with minimal effort.

Before you get going though, I encourage you to read my "Before You Start." It will make things even easier. You can use the ingredient list I provide as a help in making a shopping list and use the FAQs at the end of the section to help answer questions you might have. Additionally, you can find more helps on my website: www.MichelesGreenSmoothies.com. It's all there to help you Drink Green!

INGREDIENTS AND TIPS

I'm including the ingredient list below to help you make your shopping list. You don't have to have all of these items at the same time; my idea with this list is to give

BEFORE YOU START

Before you jump into making the smoothie recipes in this section, please take a quick look at this list—it will make your life easier!

- **Always rinse right away!** *Always rinse the pitcher and lid of your mixer within a few minutes of finishing the recipe. If you rinse them with hot water right away, you don't even have to wash them—just let them drip dry and put them away. If you don't rinse them right away, you will have to soak and scrub them by hand—they won't come clean in the dishwasher. The same thing goes for glasses you drink out of. The best time-saver for you will be to get in the habit of rinsing immediately.*
- **Try the recipes as written the first time.** *I love playing with recipes and tweaking ingredients, but I encourage you to try each recipe exactly as written the first time you make it. As I explain in my ingredients list for this section, I include ingredients in each smoothie that are meant to cancel out the flavor of the spinach. If you use significantly less spinach than called for, ingredients such as chia and coconut may come across as too strong. If you leave out chia or coconut called for in the recipe, the spinach flavor will be much more noticeable. Coconut and chia have their own potential health benefits, but they are primarily in my recipes because they make the recipes taste good while still containing a lot of greens.*
- **Add the ingredients in the order specified:** *(1) Liquids and small hard ingredients (like chia seeds and coconut); (2) soft fruit; (3) greens; and (4) frozen ingredients. The ingredients will mix better this way and may not mix at all if you don't layer them this way. If you are unsure about what your mixer can handle, you might want to start by making the 1x recipe. It's also a good idea to purée all the other ingredients before adding the spinach unless you have a high-power blender. For more information, see page 28 and the blender section on page 7.*
- **Invest in a kitchen scale.** *It simply isn't possible to be exact in measuring fruits and vegetables without having a scale, and the flavor of each of my green smoothie recipes is quite dependent on having exact measurements. You can read more about why I recommend having a kitchen scale on page 4. Until you get around to buying one (if you don't have one already), you can use my Orange Creamie Greenie and Green Grape recipes that can be measured relatively well without a scale (you will have to guesstimate on the greens using the package weight as a guide).*
- **Use baby organic spinach.** *All of my recipes call for baby spinach. You can use other greens too, but before just throwing them in, especially if you are a green smoothie novice, please read my FAQs about this on page 25.*
- **Drink the smoothie within an hour of making it.** *For best flavor, drink the smoothie within an hour of when you make it or freeze to use another day (see page 27 for more info.)*
- **In my recipes, one serving of smoothie is between 13 and 15 ounces.** *I serve my smoothies in 16-ounce glasses (adult serving).*
- **If you are new to green smoothies, work through the recipes in the order presented.** *The easiest recipes are at the start. I suggest starting with Orange Creamie Greenie.*

you an overview of what you need and give you a little more info about the more unusual items. While you don't need to get everything on this list, if you have enough freezer space and want to be equipped to try all the recipes in this section, you can buy everything on this list at the same time and cut and freeze some of the fruit for future use. The exception is the spinach. While you can freeze spinach to use in smoothies (see page 15), I think it has better flavor when used fresh, so I would recommend only buying as much baby spinach as you think you can go through in about a week, at least as you are getting started. You can find info on cutting and freezing fruit, mint, and spinach on the next pages and on my website, www.MichelesGreenSmoothies.com.

INGREDIENTS

Shelf stable

- **Dry unsweetened fine-shred coconut**—available in most grocery stores and all health food stores. Don't be afraid to try this in your smoothies even if you think you don't like coconut. Unsweetened coconut, used frequently in Europe and South America, doesn't taste much like its sweet and stringy US counterpart. It's main purpose in the smoothie is to cancel out the spinach flavor. For more on this, see page 24.

- **Chia seed** (either ground or whole)—available in most grocery stores and all health food stores. Chia has great nutritional value on its own, but I put it in my smoothie recipes mostly because of the creamy texture it adds. It also can help cancel out the "green" flavor of the greens. If you have a high-power blender I recommend getting whole chia seed. If you have a sharp-blade blender, you probably want to use ground chia. Ground chia is easier to find at health food stores while chia seed can be purchased at nearly any grocery store.

- **Vanilla extract or whole vanilla bean**—I love the flavor of vanilla and it can make your smoothies yummier than they would be otherwise!
- **Instant rolled oats or baby rice cereal**

Juices

(You can buy ready to use juices or frozen concentrate.)

- **Orange juice**
- **White grape juice**
- **Pineapple juice**
- **Apple juice**
- **Limeade** (see also page 185)

Fresh and Frozen Fruits

- **Oranges**—medium size
- **Green grapes**
- **Apples**
- **Melon** (Honeydew or Crenshaw)
- **Pears**
- **Fresh whole pineapple**—you can also get frozen pineapple chunks at some stores.
- **Bananas**

All of these except the apple and orange can be cut and frozen. Apples and oranges keep a long time in the fridge, so I don't freeze them.

Greens

- **High quality organic baby spinach** (seems to have a milder flavor than the baby spinach that isn't labeled organic). The baby organic spinach I get from some stores seems to always be fresher than spinach I get from other stores, even when it is the same brand. In picking out spinach, look for containers where the spinach seems dry (there's not a lot of extra moisture) and the leaves seem whole and undamaged. If you need to approximate spinach amounts for a smoothie, eight ounces of baby spinach are slightly more than two cups of baby spinach packed as tight as you can get it into a measuring pitcher.

- **Fresh mint sprigs**—I pick these in my garden in the summer and freeze them to use during the winter. Mint is very easy to grow. If you plant some in your yard or balcony box, expect it to take over the whole flower bed or container.

CUTTING FRUIT FOR SMOOTHIES:

I find that a lot of people have a fear of cutting fruit,and of knives in general. I learned to use knives growing up but didn't learn my favorite way to cut fruit until I worked in food service. When I first learned this fruit-cutting method, I thought it was magical. It might not be new to you, but if it is, give it a try—it can save you lots of time! Once you get this method down, you will be the one offering to cut up fruit for family parties and neighborhood baby showers because it's so easy! If you like visuals better than written instructions, visit my website for videos showing you how (www.MichelesGreenSmoothies.com.)

1. Cut both "poles" off the fruit (steps 1 and 2 in the diagram). For a pineapple, this would be the crown and the base. For an orange it would be the navel end and the stem end. If it is a large fruit like a pineapple, use a long (but narrow) knife. I usually use a serrated bread knife for pineapple. For a small fruit like an orange, use a smaller serrated knife.

2. Set the fruit on a cutting board with one of the cut ends down. This should give you a nice flat, stable surface so the fruit doesn't wiggle around while you finish cutting off the peel.

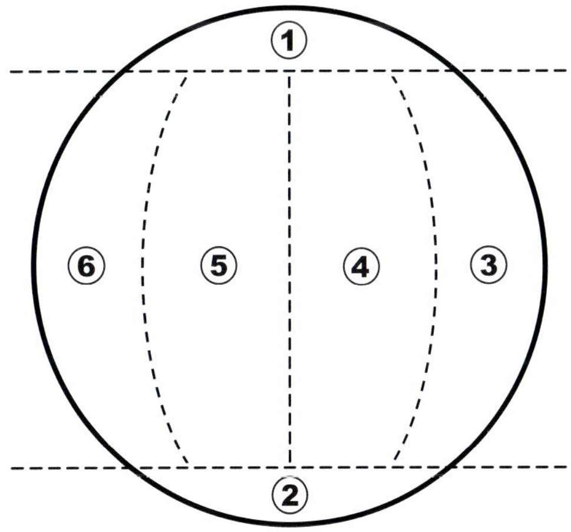

3. Make a slice down the side of the fruit, curving with the curve of the fruit. Examine the cut. It should cut away all the rind and a tiny bit of the fruit. If you aren't happy with the depth of your cut, adjust the next cut. Work your way around the fruit, cutting off strips of rind or peel. Cut from top to bottom and turn the fruit after each cut until you have gone all the way around (other steps in the diagram).

4. Discard the rind or peel to get it out of the way. If you are cutting a pineapple, quarter it, cutting from top to bottom, then cut out the core. If you are cutting a melon like honeydew, cut it in half, top to bottom, then scoop out the seeds. When cutting pineapple for smoothies or a fruit tray, I remove the core as described above, then cut each quarter in half the long way (the pineapple is now in eight sections). I then cut each of these long sections into 1-inch wide pieces. If cutting a melon, I remove the seeds and then flip the melon half over so it is flat and stable on the cutting board. I then make several cuts straight down through the melon in both directions, cutting the melon into cubes (more or less).

For an orange I cut the orange in half, place the flat cut sides down and then cut it smaller as needed (depends on your blender.)

Tips

- When cutting fruit, people are often afraid of cutting too much away. If you have issues with this, take a moment and think about pineapple rings in a can. How did they get the shape they are? Only by cutting a lot off of the outside. When you cut your pineapple, even if you cut deep enough to get all of the rind off, you will still be leaving much more pineapple than the cutting machines do, and you will be saving money because you are cutting it yourself. So don't be afraid to cut off what you need to for the fruit to look and taste good—whether it's pineapple, melon, or oranges.
- If you are new to this method, practice on an orange until you get the hang of it. If it doesn't seem to be working well, try a different knife.

FREEZING FRUIT FOR SMOOTHIES

I love having frozen fruit for smoothies because it makes it so easy to throw a smoothie together and means I don't need as much ice. Remember when you use frozen fruit to add it to the smoothie last—it will blend in easier if everything else is already liquefied.

I have two methods for freezing fruit:

Method One: Cut the fruit to the size you want it. Drop it into a gallon zip-seal bag, filling the bag no more than half full. Seal the bag and then lay it flat. Arrange the fruit so it is all in a single layer and place it in the freezer like that. Once the fruit is frozen you can stand the bag up. If the pieces are stuck to each other too much, bang the bag once on the counter to break them apart.

Method Two: Line a baking pan with plastic wrap or with a reusable pan liner (like Silpat.) Spread the pieces of fruit evenly on the pan and place it in the freezer. Once the fruit is frozen, you can bag it. If pieces are stuck to each other or to the pan, bang the pan on the counter to loosen them.

Here are some specific instructions for each kind of fruit I use:

- **Oranges:** I generally don't cut and freeze my oranges for smoothies because oranges keep so well whole and aren't that hard to peel. If you want to freeze them, cut the peel off as instructed above, then slice into chunks. You can also peel them by hand, break them into sections, and freeze using method one or two above.
- **Grapes:** I do grapes a couple ways. If I am preparing grapes to eat fresh, I cut the grapes into bunches, rinse them thoroughly, and then freeze the grapes that fell off the stems during washing to use for smoothies. If you want to freeze a lot of grapes, you will need to pick them off the stems—the stems will not grind up, even in a high power blender. Rinse them, let them drip dry, and then put them in a bag.
- **Apples:** Apples don't freeze well and are super easy to cut. I don't recommend freezing them.
- **Pineapple:** Cut as directed above and then freeze using method one or two. If using it for smoothies, you can

leave the core on if desired when cutting it into pieces. One pineapple yields about two pounds of cut fruit.

- **Melon:** Cut as directed above and then freeze the cubes using method one or method two above.
- **Pears:** My favorite way to cut pears is using an apple cutter—the kind you push down and it cuts the apple into segments and removes the core. I like to freeze pears when they are available in the fall. Freeze using method one or two above.
- **Bananas:** Wait until your bananas start to get "freckles." At this point they are at their peak sweetness but haven't started going bad. I like to rinse my bananas before peeling them. Peel the bananas and cut each one into four pieces. I like to use method two above for bananas because they bruise so easily. Handle them as little as possible as you are cutting them and placing them on the tray and they will keep better.

Grapes, pineapple, and melon will keep for over a year frozen. Pears will last a year, but will start to go brown. Bananas will start to go brown after a few months in the freezer.

STORING AND FREEZING SPINACH AND MINT:

Refrigerator

Here are some things I do to help my baby spinach keep longer in the fridge:

- I usually buy my spinach in one-pound containers. After I take some out and put the lid back on, I shake the container to loosen the remaining leaves and redistribute any moisture. I usually store it upside-down so that moisture will tend to flow away from the leaves that were sitting in the bottom of the container at the store. If there seems to be a lot of moisture in the container I place half a paper towel in the top before I close it. Since the top will become the bottom, the towel can help absorb moisture.
- If I purchase two one-pound containers at the same time, I use half of the first container, shake it, and store it upside-down as mentioned above. Then I use half of the other container and do the same thing. This will help both containers of spinach keep longer.
- If you have larger leaf spinach or Swiss chard from your garden or from the store, wash it, trim the stems, and then stand it in a cup of water like you would do with cut flowers. Store in the refrigerator. This also works well for cut stems of mint.

Freezer

As I mentioned before, I think spinach gets a little stronger flavor when frozen. I also think it is harder to mix into the smoothies when frozen if you are also using frozen fruit; however, it can be very convenient. A friend of mine likes to pre-measure the fruit and spinach for a smoothie in a bag so that she can just pull out the bag and dump it in the blender with the juice or water and other ingredients. If you have a powerful blender, you could certainly do this. To freeze spinach, just put it in a bag in the freezer. After it is frozen, it will crumble, so you can crush the bag and have it take less space. It thaws very quickly and becomes mushy, so if you do freeze it, pre-measuring is a good idea so you don't have to leave the bag out while you weigh it.

If you grow your own mint, you can pick it in the summer and freeze it to use for the winter. If you buy mint and don't use it all at once, you can also freeze it.

Tips

- If you are washing the mint, dry it well before freezing.
- Place mint sprigs in an airtight container in the freezer. Use as needed. Keeps for several months to a year.

orange creamie greenie

This is one of my favorite green smoothie recipes. It reminds me of a Creamsicle and is great for beginners. It is a good one to do during the winter when oranges are in season.

INGREDIENTS	1X	2X
orange juice	6 oz.	12 oz.
fresh orange, peel removed	½ of a medium orange, about 2 oz.	1 medium orange or about 4 oz.
chia or ground chia	1 Tbsp.	2 Tbsp.
unsweetened coconut	2 Tbsp.	¼ cup
vanilla extract or vanilla bean	1 tsp. or ¼ bean	2 tsp. or ½ bean
baby spinach	4 oz.	8 oz.
ice	2–3 cubes	4–6 cubes
Serves:	1	2

INSTRUCTIONS

1. Measure the orange juice into the mixing carafe. Cut the peel from the orange and cut the orange into quarters. Add to the carafe.

2. Measure and add the chia, coconut, and vanilla.

3. Set the carafe on your kitchen scale and "zero" the scale. Add the indicated weight of greens and then the ice cubes.

4. Blend until mixture is completely smooth and all one color. Drink within the next hour or freeze to use another day.

TIPS AND VARIATIONS

- Visit my website for a video on how to cut the peel from the orange (www.MichelesGreenSmoothies.com.) If you have large oranges, use ½ of an orange for the 2x batch.
- This recipe tastes best with both chia and coconut (both ingredients that cancel out the spinach flavor) but tastes okay with just chia).
- Orange-Banana: use banana instead of the orange. (Still use orange juice.)
- Orange-Pineapple: substitute pineapple for the orange.
- Holiday Eggnog: Instead of the 12 ounces orange juice in the 2x recipe, use 8 ounces eggnog and 4 ounces orange juice. Add a dash of cinnamon if desired. Coconut and chia are optional. Not as healthy perhaps, but yummy and festive! Even if you don't like eggnog, you may like it in this combination; just make sure you get good eggnog. Our favorite is Southern Comfort brand Cinnamon Vanilla eggnog.

The ingredients shown in the photo are the amounts needed for the 2X recipe.

green grape

This has a light, sweet flavor and is a good one for beginners. It is green grape, so it should be green!

INGREDIENTS	1X	2X
white grape juice	4 oz.	8 oz.
chia or ground chia	1 Tbsp.	2 Tbsp.
unsweetened coconut	1–2 Tbsp.	2–4 Tbsp.
fresh green grapes	3–4 oz. (17–25 grapes)	6–8 oz. (35–50 grapes)
baby spinach	4 oz.	8 oz.
ice	2–3 cubes	4–6 cubes
Serves:	1	2

INSTRUCTIONS

1. Measure the grape juice into the mixing carafe and add the chia, coconut, and grapes.

2. Set the carafe on your kitchen scale and "zero" the scale. Add the indicated weight of greens and then the ice cubes.

3. Blend until mixture is completely smooth and all one color. Drink within the next hour or freeze to use another day.

TIPS AND VARIATIONS

- This smoothie is quite sweet. You can make it less sweet by using water instead of some of the grape juice or by adding a squeeze of fresh lime juice. I suggest using the juice from about a quarter of a lime for the 1x recipe.
- You can use the grapes fresh as called for in the recipe, or wash them and freeze them. If you use frozen grapes, add a little water with the grape juice and use the frozen grapes instead of ice.
- It is possible to use grapes with seeds, and people say that grape seeds are good for you, but I don't like the grainy texture of the seeds in the smoothie, even if the smoothie is made with a high-power blender.

simple apple

This simple smoothie tastes like apple but mostly it just tastes "fresh." It has a nice fluffy texture because of the air in the apple (apples "bob" because they are about 25 percent air.)

INGREDIENTS	1X	2X
water or apple juice	6 oz.	12 oz.
chia or ground chia	1 Tbsp.	2 Tbsp.
unsweetened coconut	1 Tbsp.	2 Tbsp.
fresh apple, core removed	5 oz., about 1 medium apple	10 oz., about 2 medium apples
baby spinach	4 oz.	8 oz.
ice cubes	3–4 cubes	6–8 cubes
Serves:	1	2

INSTRUCTIONS

1. Measure the water or apple juice into the mixing carafe. Measure and add the chia and coconut.

2. Set the carafe on your kitchen scale and "zero" the scale. Add the indicated weight of apple (sectioned and with core removed). "Zero" the scale again and add the indicated weight of greens. Add the ice cubes.

3. Blend until mixture is completely smooth and all one color. Drink within the next hour or freeze to use another day.

pineapple mint green suco

Nearly every juice bar in Rio offers a refreshing juice blend of fresh pineapple with fresh mint. When you add greens, the mint does a great job of helping to mask their flavor and, with the fresh mint flavor, the color seems appropriate.

INGREDIENTS	1X	2X
pineapple juice	6 oz.	12 oz.
unsweetened coconut	2–3 Tbsp.	¼–⅓ cup
fresh or frozen mint sprigs	1 sprig	2 sprigs
baby spinach	4 oz.	8 oz.
fresh or frozen pineapple	3 oz.	6 oz.
ice as needed	2–3 cubes	4–6 cubes
Serves:	1	2

INSTRUCTIONS

1. Measure the pineapple juice into the mixing carafe. Add the coconut and mint.

2. Set the carafe on your kitchen scale and "zero" the scale. Add the indicated weight of greens. Zero the scale again and then add the indicated weight of fresh or frozen pineapple. Add the ice if not using frozen pineapple.

3. Blend until mixture is completely smooth and all one color. Drink within the next hour or freeze to use another day.

TIPS AND VARIATIONS

- If using frozen pineapple, you can add water instead of ice—2 ounces for the 1x recipe, 4 ounces for the 2x recipe.
- It can be hard to know how much mint to add and mint sprigs as they come in the grocery store vary a lot in size. The photo shows the amount of mint I generally use for the 2X recipe. If you get somewhere around this amount your smoothie will be fine—a little more or less is okay too.
- You can use frozen pineapple juice concentrate plus water instead of pineapple juice. For the 2x recipe use 3–4 ounces concentrate plus water to equal 12 ounces liquid. For stronger pineapple flavor, use more concentrate and less water. You can also leave out the mint, add some chia, and have this as a "Dole Whip" pineapple smoothie. For 2x recipe, add 2 tablespoons chia.
- To make this as a refreshing Brazilian drink without greens, just use water, pineapple, ice, and a little bit of fresh mint.

melão com limão

In Brazil there are two words for melon—melancia, *which is watermelon, and* melão, *which is everything else. Just about any non-watermelon melon will work in this recipe. I prefer varieties that are similar to honeydew or crenshaw (and are green or yellow), but cantaloupe works okay too. The sweeter the melon, the better the smoothie will be. Lime (limão) enhances the flavor of the melon and helps mask the flavor of the greens.*

INGREDIENTS	1X	2X
Limeade—see Note	6 oz.	12 oz.
chia or ground chia	1 Tbsp.	2 Tbsp.
unsweetened coconut	2 Tbsp.	¼ cup
baby spinach	4 oz.	8 oz.
frozen melon chunks	4 oz.	8 oz.
Serves:	1	2

INSTRUCTIONS

1. Measure the limeade into the mixing carafe.

2. Measure and add the chia and coconut.

3. Set the carafe on your kitchen scale and "zero" the scale. Add the indicated weight of greens and then the indicated weight of frozen melon chunks.

4. Blend until mixture is completely smooth and all one color. Drink within the next hour or freeze to use another day.

Note: You can make your own limeade concentrate (see page 185) or use frozen limeade concentrate. You can also make this recipe using water instead of limeade. If using water, add ½–1 tablespoon honey and ½ of a lime wedge with the peel on (about 1/12 of a lime) for the 1x recipe.

TIPS AND VARIATIONS

- Melon has a very high water content, so I recommend using frozen melon instead of fresh so that the flavor isn't diluted by needing to add ice cubes. For tips on freezing melon for smoothies, see page 14.
- Although melon seeds are edible and apparently very nutritious, I like this recipe much better with just the melon—no seeds.

honey pear

Honey enhances the pear flavor in this delicious smoothie!

INGREDIENTS	1X	2X
water	6 oz.	12 oz.
honey	1 Tbsp.	2 Tbsp.
vanilla extract (optional)	½ tsp.	1 tsp.
unsweetened coconut	1–2 Tbsp.	2–4 Tbsp.
chia or ground chia	½ Tbsp.	1 Tbsp.
fresh or frozen ripe pears, stem and seeds removed.	6 oz.	12 oz.
baby spinach	5 oz.	10 oz.
ice cubes if needed	3–4 cubes	6–8 cubes
Serves:	1	2

INSTRUCTIONS

1. Measure the water and honey into the mixing carafe. Measure and add the vanilla (if desired), coconut, and chia.

2. Set the carafe on your kitchen scale and "zero" the scale. Add the indicated weight of pear (remove stem and seeds) and the indicated weight of greens. Add ice cubes if not using frozen pear.

3. Blend until mixture is completely smooth and all one color. Drink within the next hour or freeze to use another day.

TIPS AND VARIATIONS

- A fun variation is to use Elderflower concentrate. Elderflower concentrate is available in bottles at Ikea and is called *Saft Flaeder*. It is a typical drink throughout Europe, but especially in Sweden and Austria. Use 1 ounce of concentrate with 5 ounces water in the 1x recipe and leave out the honey. The Elderflower flavor compliments the pear very nicely.
- You can also try white grape juice in this recipe instead of honey and water.

brazilian-style banana milk shake

The "Banana com Farinha Lactea Vitamina" was my husband's favorite drink to get at juice bars when he lived in Brazil. Farinha Lactea is a popular instant hot breakfast cereal for adults and children in Brazil and is commonly added to certain kinds of smoothies. If you have Farinha Lactea on hand (or better still, whole grain Farinha Lactea), you can use it instead of the oats or baby rice cereal and the vanilla called for in this recipe. This version adds greens but tastes similar.

INGREDIENTS	1X	2X
orange juice	6 oz.	12 oz.
quick oats or baby rice cereal	2 Tbsp.	¼ cup
unsweetened coconut	2 Tbsp.	¼ cup
chia or ground chia (optional)	½ Tbsp.	1 Tbsp.
vanilla extract or vanilla bean	1 tsp. or ¼ bean	2 tsp. or ½ bean
baby spinach	4 oz.	8 oz.
frozen banana chunks	4 oz.	8 oz.
Serves:	1	2

INSTRUCTIONS

1. Measure the orange juice into the mixing carafe.

2. Measure and add the oats or baby rice cereal, coconut, chia (if desired), and vanilla.

3. Set the carafe on your kitchen scale and "zero" the scale. Add the indicated weight of greens. Zero the scale again and add the indicated weight of frozen banana chunks.

4. Blend until mixture is completely smooth and all one color. Drink within the next hour or freeze to use another day.

TIPS AND VARIATIONS

- Despite the use of orange juice, this recipe tastes primarily of banana. If you prefer, instead of orange juice you can use the following as a base (1x recipe): ¼ cup water, ½ cup kefir, 2–3 small dates (pits removed). Blend these together until dates disappear, then add the other ingredients. You can try using this base recipe with other smoothies in this book as well.
- Freeze the bananas for this recipe when they have started to get "freckles." For more tips on freezing fruit for smoothies, see page 14.
- If you like banana milk shake, make the recipe as it is. If don't love bananas, try adding half of a lime wedge (1⁄12 of a lime) to the 1x recipe or squeezing in some lime or lemon juice. It will still taste delicious, but will have a lighter banana flavor.
- Also tastes good using half banana and half pineapple for the fruit.

FREQUENTLY ASKED QUESTIONS

DO YOU ALWAYS DRINK YOUR SMOOTHIES FOR BREAKFAST?

I do, and I have a couple reasons. The main one is that breakfast is the hardest meal for me to bring vegetables and greens into. It's common in other countries, like Turkey and many Middle Eastern countries, to have some tomatoes or cucumbers or lettuce for breakfast, but that's not really typical in the United States. For me, drinking a fruit smoothie with greens is the easiest and most comfortable way to get vegetables into breakfast. I also feel that breakfast is the meal of the day that most people—including me—care the least about in terms of having variety. Lots of people will eat the same breakfast nearly every day or rotate through maybe two or three with a special breakfast on the weekend. I enjoy the ease of knowing what I'm making for breakfast each day (a smoothie), I enjoy how quick my smoothies are to prepare and I enjoy how satisfied I feel for hours after drinking a full serving. Some people run to the grocery store in the evening or early morning because they have run out of milk for their cereal. I run to the grocery store when I run out of spinach for my smoothie!

SOME PEOPLE I KNOW MAKE A GREEN SMOOTHIE AND DRINK IT FOR BREAKFAST, LUNCH, AND DINNER OR JUST SIP AT IT ALL DAY. DO YOU EVER DO THAT?

I think I'm too much of a foodie to do that. I like variety. I enjoy trying all the different flavors and textures and combinations of food there are. Vegetables and fruits in particular have so much variety! I think its fun to try new ones or old ones in new ways—once you start liking them.

Now that I have been drinking smoothies for a few years, there are days that I need an easy portable lunch and a smoothie sounds like the best thing. That doesn't happen too often and happens most often on days that I am really craving greens and just can't seem to get enough. Having a green smoothie for lunch on those days is easy and leaves me satisfied, but I couldn't have done that a couple years ago—it just wouldn't have sounded good.

I don't sip smoothies throughout the day like some people do. I think the flavor quality of almost any green smoothie goes downhill with time, so I would rather drink a freshly made smoothie. When I drink a full serving of smoothie for breakfast I'm usually not hungry for at least a couple of hours (usually longer). If I do feel hungry when I finish my smoothie, I will sometimes have a slice of bread or a handful of nuts or one of my Puffy Whole-Grain Pancakes that I have frozen.

WHY DO ALL OF YOUR SMOOTHIES CALL FOR SPINACH AND COCONUT?

I use spinach in my smoothies in combination with coconut because spinach and coconut so neatly, and nearly completely, cancel each other out in terms of flavor. When I was experimenting with green smoothies, I found that if a smoothie tasted too "spinach-y," if I added a little more coconut that spinach-y flavor went away. Adding more coconut didn't boost the coconut flavor, just neutralized the green flavor of the spinach. This effect doesn't seem to happen with other greens, so that's why I usually stick with spinach for the smoothies (more on this below.) Spinach has what I call a "green" flavor but not much of a bitter flavor like some other greens have. Coconut seems to have no effect on greens such as kale and lettuce that have a bitter flavor. I did experiments with other coconut products such as coconut water, coconut oil, and coconut flour but these didn't have the same neutralizing effect.

WHAT IF I MADE THE RECIPE AS WRITTEN BUT THE SMOOTHIE STILL HAS A STRONG SPINACH FLAVOR?

I've noticed that some batches of baby organic spinach seem to have a stronger spinach flavor than others. If I make a smoothie and it has a strong spinach flavor, I usually add another tablespoon or two of coconut and blend it again (adding extra ice if needed.) If I make another smoothie with that same batch of spinach, I add extra coconut to start with.

I'VE HAD (OR MADE) SMOOTHIES WITH OTHER GREENS BESIDES SPINACH THAT TASTED GOOD. WHY DO YOU SAY SPINACH WORKS BEST?

In my experience, if I find a smoothie recipe that call for greens other than spinach and tastes good, it generally has proportionally much less in the way of greens than my recipes do or has other ingredients I'm trying to minimize (see page 80). The main point of my smoothies is to increase the amount of greens in the smoothie as much as possible and use almost all fruit and vegetable ingredients. That's why I refer to them as "intensely green" smoothies.

IF I WANT TO BRANCH OUT AND TRY SOME OTHER GREENS IN MY SMOOTHIES, ARE THERE ANY YOU WOULD RECOMMEND?

I think the leaves of baby bok choi are quite mild and also the leaf part of Swiss chard if you remove the stem. When I use bok choi or chard I use it 50/50 with spinach. Some stores sell a combination of baby bok choi, baby chard, and baby kale that has only a very mild bitter flavor. These baby-greens mixes are usually packaged with a label something like "power greens." *Mâche*, a.k.a. field salad, can also work well but it's hard to find in the United States.

WHY DO YOU FEEL IT'S SO IMPORTANT TO INCREASE THE AMOUNT OF GREENS IN ONE'S DIET?

Most of my life I have had mild to moderate problems with hypoglycemia (low blood sugar). I particularly had problems if I ate a lot of sugary food or simple carbohydrates. I found that my body did much better on a high protein diet, but my gut feeling was that eating a lot of meat, eggs, and dairy was not going to be the best for my health long term. When I found out that greens have (per calorie) a very high amount of protein, and lots and lots of needed nutrients, I thought that might solve my problem. Since I started eating a greens-heavy diet, problems with hypoglycemia have become a thing of the past for me, except when I don't get enough greens. Eating and drinking green has also helped significantly with other health problems I have such as irritable bowel syndrome and insomnia. Not everyone has health problems, but I think eating and drinking green can help anyone have a healthier body and help prevent health problems that would arise in the future.

I HAVE HEARD THAT IT IS IMPORTANT TO EAT A VARIETY OF GREENS. AREN'T YOU WORRIED THAT YOU ARE GETTING TOO MUCH SPINACH BY HAVING SPINACH SMOOTHIES?

My feeling is that since I am usually eating some greens at every meal, and only have spinach for breakfast (in my smoothies) I am getting a fairly balanced variety of greens over the course of a day or a week. I don't have any recipes in this book (other than the smoothie recipes) that call for spinach and that is why: I want to use the spinach where it is most useful (in smoothies) and balance it with other greens at other meals. As an example of how I do this, I usually have 4 ounces of spinach in a smoothie for breakfast, 2–3 ounces of other greens for lunch and 4–6 ounces of other greens or raw vegetables for dinner. This is where I think it is very important to listen to your body. When a smoothie sounds completely unappetizing to me, I have something else instead that day for breakfast. Sometimes I will go two or three days without having a green smoothie because it just sounds unappealing. By the third or fourth day, I am craving a smoothie again and it tastes delicious when I make one.

I'VE HEARD SPINACH IS HIGH IN OXALATES. IS THAT A PROBLEM?

It is true that spinach is high in oxalates; however oxalates in the diet are a problem for a very, very small subsection of people and those people usually know who they are. Oxalates actually occur naturally in a huge variety of foods and are also made in the body; for some reason though, most people only know about oxalates in connection with spinach. The majority of the population of the United States are at risk for diseases that can be helped or avoided by eating a diet high in fiber, nutrients and green vegetables. Very few will have a problem with oxalates. For a good summary of the information on this visit: http://www.whfoods.com/genpage.php?tname=george&dbid=48.

DID YOU HAVE ANY PROBLEM ADJUSTING TO EATING SO MANY GREENS?

Yes. When my husband and I changed our eating plan, we had some nausea and indigestion for two to three months. After that, our bodies seemed to adjust. I recommend starting slowly with green smoothies. I think if I knew then what I do now (and had my yummy smoothie recipes) I would start with a half serving of green smoothie three days a week and stick with that for about a month. Then, if I felt like my body was used to that, I would increase to a full serving three days a week for a month. At that point I would say "listen to your body." If it makes your stomach turn to think about having a smoothie on a certain day, skip it.

CAN I USE UP GREENS THAT ARE STARTING TO GO BAD BY PUTTING THEM IN A SMOOTHIE?

I am always sad when food goes bad before I can use it, but greens that go bad really taste awful and won't taste any better in a smoothie—in fact they will taste worse. When I have greens go bad and have to throw them away, I try not to think about it in terms of monetary cost but of environmental impact. The amount of resources that go into producing greens is much less than almost any other food product. If you have to throw greens away, you could think of it like sweeping up the fall leaves or grass clippings to put in the compost. (You can of course also put greens that have gotten away from you in your composter if you have one.) I sometimes give greens or ends of lettuce heads to my neighbor who has a tortoise. If you have a lot of greens go bad when you first start trying to eat green, don't give up; with time and experience you will get better at keeping them and using them when they need to be used.

WHY DO YOU CALL FOR FRUIT JUICES IN YOUR SMOOTHIES? I THOUGHT FRUIT JUICES SHOULD BE AVOIDED?

Fruit juice contains fructose, a type of sugar that occurs naturally in fruits. Juices typically contain little or no fiber. When you drink fruit juice straight, it is easy for the sugars in the juice to have a strong effect on blood sugar because the fiber isn't there to slow down it's absorption. The other problem with fruit juice is that it is usually pasteurized, which means that it has been heated and the heat will have decreased the amount of vitamins available to your body. I find that my smoothies taste better when they are a little sweeter than they would be with just water. Juice is an easy way to provide that extra sweetness and adds an extra flavor boost as well. My smoothies have a lot of fiber, so I'm not really concerned about the sugars from the juice being absorbed too quickly. As you get used to the smoothies, you can decrease the amount of juice you use and replace it with water if you want to, or you can use my date smoothie base (see page 23.)

DO YOU USE ANY SPECIAL KIND OF WATER IN YOUR SMOOTHIES? WHAT KIND OF WATER DO YOU DRINK?

I use filtered tap water in my smoothies, but I drink alkaline water that I get from a water store. On an intellectual level, I don't actually believe in alkaline water or in most of the claims that are made about the various types of water marketed today. That being said, a couple years ago I gave alkaline water a try for a month and found it tasted better to me. I go out of my way to buy it and drink it whenever I can because I have found it is easier for me to drink more of it and I do believe it is important to drink enough water. When I have alkaline water around, I will routinely drink two full glasses first thing in the morning—something I could never get myself to do with tap water or filtered water. If you are one of those people who knows you should drink more water but can't get yourself to, I would encourage you to visit a water store and try some of the different kinds. If one seems to go down easier, try it for a month. You can also try my mint water recipe (page 188).

CAN I USE OTHER COCONUT PRODUCTS IN MY SMOOTHIE, LIKE COCONUT WATER?

It certainly won't hurt to use coconut water in your smoothie instead of water, but you still need the finely shredded coconut to cancel the green flavor of the spinach. I tried using coconut oil, coconut water, and coconut flour instead of the finely shredded coconut and none of them had the same effect.

SOME GREEN SMOOTHIE BOOKS RECOMMEND "CHEWING" YOUR SMOOTHIE AS YOU DRINK IT TO AID ITS DIGESTION. WHAT DO YOU THINK ABOUT THIS?

I think it's probably good advice. I don't always do it myself though.

YOU SAY THAT YOUR SMOOTHIES TASTE BETTER FRESHLY MADE. IS THERE ANY GOOD WAY TO KEEP SOME FOR ANOTHER DAY?

Yes! Freezing them works great. I freeze smoothies in 16-ounce containers. If I want one to be ready to drink for breakfast, I put the frozen smoothie in an insulated lunch bag just before I go to bed. By morning it is mostly thawed but still cold (when kept at standard room temperature). Here's another method that is quicker: Bring some water to a boil. Remove the water from the heat and submerge one or two smoothie bottles in the hot water. Leave them for ten minutes. Shake the smoothie(s) vigorously. Return the smoothie(s) to the now warm water for an additional ten minutes. Shake vigorously and enjoy. (Note: the center may still be frozen at this point but should continue to thaw as you drink it. If your bottle is fatter than about 2-inches diameter, it will take longer than indicated here for the center to thaw.)

I NEED TO MAKE MORE SMOOTHIE EVERY DAY THAN I CAN EASILY MAKE IN MY BLENDER AND DON'T LIKE HAVING TO DO TWO BATCHES. DO YOU HAVE ANY SUGGESTIONS?

Almost every make of blender has the option of buying a replacement carafe. If you buy a second carafe (with blade), it makes things easier because you can measure the ingredients into both carafes at the same time, then place them on the machine part to blend, one after the other. This can also be a great way to make extra smoothies to freeze and use another day.

I'M GOING ON VACATION BUT STILL WANT TO HAVE MY GREEN SMOOTHIES. DO YOU HAVE ANY SUGGESTIONS?

If I'm going on a trip in the car, I will often take my blender and the dry ingredients like coconut and chia with me. While on the trip I plan to make recipes that use orange, apple, or grape (fruits that are easy to use fresh and don't require refrigeration). I pick up greens as I need them at grocery stores and keep them in an ice chest or hotel fridge. I usually take a refrigerator thermometer along so I can make sure the hotel fridge won't freeze my spinach and any other fresh veggies or fruits I may be taking. Most hotels provide ice and disposable cups, so that part is no problem.

When going on a trip where I will be flying, I plan on checking a bag and take frozen smoothies in a lunch-size insulated bag with an ice pack. I store them in the freezing compartment of the hotel fridge until ready to use. If its a longer trip, I spread the smoothies out over the days I will be gone and try to eat a big salad on the other days.

WHY DON'T YOU ADD "X", "Y," OR "Z" TO YOUR SMOOTHIES?

There are lots of people who add lots of things to their smoothies—everything from protein powder to so-called superfoods to a variety of vegetables. Science says that greens are one of the most, if not the most nutritionally dense foods on the planet (among other studies, see the list here: http://www.washingtonpost.com/news/to-your-health/wp/2014/06/05/finally-a-list-of-powerhouse-fruits-and-vegetables-ranked-by-how-much-nutrition-they-contain/). I feel that maximizing the greens is the most important thing I can do with my smoothies. That, and keeping them tasting good so that I will drink them. I've had the most success keeping my smoothies delicious by keeping them simple and using unsweetened coconut.

MY MIXER DOESN'T SEEM TO BE HANDLING BLENDING THE GREENS VERY WELL. DO YOU HAVE ANY SUGGESTIONS?

If you are layering as directed in the recipe and your blender doesn't seem to have the power to pull the greens down into the liquids to purée them, I suggest weighing your greens in a separate container and then adding them to the mixer a handful at a time, making sure to run the mixer in between handfuls. Add the next handful after the previous handful is incorporated into the liquids.

If you find that the smoothie's texture is chunky or grainy, I would run the blender again until the smoothie is truly smooth—that's how my recipes are meant to be served. If you have a high-power blender (with blunt blades, not sharp—see page 7) running the blender longer will create enough friction to heat up the smoothie a little, so you may need to add more ice.

YOU SAY THAT I CAN JUST RINSE MY BLENDER PITCHER AND LID WITH HOT WATER, BUT IT SEEMS LIKE THEY AREN'T GETTING REALLY CLEAN. WHAT DO YOU RECOMMEND?

There are several things to consider in connection with getting a blender pitcher clean. Here's a list of questions you can ask yourself:

- Does the blade come out for cleaning? If yes, you should take it apart to rinse it. Same thing with the lid. All parts that can come apart should be taken apart for rinsing.
- Did the recipe contain any oil or oily ingredients? If so, you will need to use soap and hot water, not just hot water. Soap is specifically designed to remove oils and really doesn't do anything else, so if the recipe contains only ingredients that are safe to eat raw and doesn't have really oily ingredients, hot water should do the job.

- Are you letting the pitcher, lid, blade, and assembly get really dry before the next use? If you rinse your pitcher and then let it sit with a puddle of water in it, bacteria could grow in the water since it could have a slight residue of smoothie.

I usually rinse my blender pitcher and lid with hot water every time I make a green smoothie and put it through the dishwasher once a week to remove anything that I didn't get rinsed well during the week. If I use my blender to make a sauce containing oil or my Great Fruit Smoothie, which contains coconut oil (page 186), I wash the blender pitcher and lid with soap.

DO YOU HAVE ANY SUGGESTIONS ON GETTING KIDS TO LIKE GREEN SMOOTHIES?

I think one of the most helpful things can be to involve kids in making the smoothies. My four-year-old nephew enjoys helping to add the ingredients and tasting or smelling the various ingredients as they are added. One time we blended all the base ingredients for Orange Creamie Greenie and let him taste the base before adding the greens. I asked him if he could tell that the base had some of the orange he had tasted and the vanilla he had smelled. After a couple tastes, he decided he really liked the base and we poured some in a cup for him. We then added the spinach to the remaining base (cutting the amount back to account for the missing base) and when it was done, poured some of the green smoothie in a cup. He enjoyed comparing the taste of the base and the finished smoothie and noticing that the flavor hadn't really changed—only the color. He enjoyed pouring some of the green smoothie into his cup of light orange base and seeing how the color changed.

I think the most important thing can be to not try to trick kids into drinking it or force them. If this topic is of interest to you, I highly recommend reading the book *French Kids Eat Everything* by Karen Le Billon. While it doesn't cover green smoothies, it does talk a lot about how to develop a taste for vegetables in babies, children, and adults. It's an easy and fun read—I read it in one afternoon because I couldn't put it down—and I think it gives some of the most sound and useful advice I have ever read on the topic.

ARE THERE ANY INGREDIENTS YOU TRIED OUT THAT YOU WOULDN'T RECOMMEND USING IN A GREEN SMOOTHIE?

I tested every type of fruit readily available in my smoothies. I was often surprised at which ones didn't work out for me. Here is a list of fruits tested, but not approved:

- **Peach**—I love peach in fruit smoothies, but when I added the greens, it no longer tasted like peach. As my husband aptly put it, "It tastes like you put the whole peach branch in the blender." Some people say they love peach in their intensely green smoothies though, so feel free to experiment.
- **Mango**—same as peach.
- **Strawberry**—surprisingly, this was one of the worst, if not *the* worst combination I tried. It looked and tasted basically like mud—no hint of either strawberry or spinach flavor—just "yuck."
- **Blueberry**—turns the smoothie color brown and has no blueberry flavor. I tried boosting the flavor by adding dried blueberries, but it still just tasted kind of "muddy."
- **Kiwi**—I have a hard time finding kiwis that are truly ripe and sweet and ripening them on the counter never seems to get them where I would like them. The kiwi smoothies I made were okay and tasted vaguely of kiwi, but it didn't seem worth the effort. (I peeled and

froze the kiwis). If you find good kiwis and want to try it, follow the Basic Apple Recipe, substituting kiwi for apple.

- **Apricot**—kind of a "muddy" flavor.
- **Plum/plum cinnamon**—plum cinnamon is a common combination in Germany and tastes delicious, but when I used it in a smoothie, the flavor didn't come through.
- **Mixed berries**—okay, but not great. Other recipes say "add berries, and it will turn your smoothie purple." My experience says it will turn your smoothie brown and never really taste like berries.
- **Guava paste** (available in Latin American supermarkets)—tastes quite good in a smoothie. I didn't include it because it often contains questionable preservatives and only tastes good when drunk immediately. If you want to try it, the 1x recipe is as follows: 6 ounces water, 2 ounces guava paste, 1 tablespoon chia, 2 tablespoon unsweetened coconut, 4 ounces spinach and 3–5 ice cubes.

In addition to the fruits mentioned above, I tried adding various spices to my intensely green smoothies. I also tried various flavor extracts and cocoa. Except for vanilla, I found that most of these additions didn't help. They came across as out of place and unnatural, even with extensive testing.

SECTION 2

Salads

- SALADS ARE EXCITING!
- INGREDIENTS AND TIPS
- RECIPES
- USING UNUSUAL VEGETABLES, FRUITS, AND GREENS
- FREQUENTLY ASKED QUESTIONS

SALADS ARE EXCITING!

The biggest and nicest array of salads I have ever seen was at a high-end buffet at a resort on the Red Sea on the Gulf of Aqaba. The variety of vegetable and fruit dishes was truly amazing. They tasted fresh, were beautifully presented, and just kept going. Traveling in the Middle East I found generally there were lots of good salads—even at small falafel stands in more out-of-the-way towns. What really surprised and impressed me though was the presence of tomatoes, cucumbers, and other vegetables at breakfast. It had never occurred to me to think of fresh vegetables as breakfast food, and it was one of the experiences that, years later, would make me more receptive to the idea of green smoothies for breakfast.

As I have seen and eaten salads in Europe, Brazil, and other places, I have come to appreciate more just how much variety there is in the edible part of the plant kingdom. I had always regarded with wonder the various types of flowers (I used to do flower arranging) but began to see just how much beauty and flavor and color could be found in vegetables.

I don't seem to be alone in noticing this. Celebrity chefs now commonly make dishes with names like "Grilled Squid with Avocado, Watermelon, and Endive" or "Pan-seared Trout with Summer Corn, Tomatoes, and Grapes." In these dishes the seafood takes a backseat, and it is the vegetables and fruits with their assorted colors and textures that are really on display.

With so much variety in vegetables and fruits to choose from, there are endless variations in salad-making. In this section I could only scratch the surface of possible salads, so I chose recipes that represented a type of salad or a concept in salad-making. I start with more familiar types of salads and move into salads that have ingredients or methods that are slightly more adventurous. At the end, I provide a list of vegetables and fruits you may not have thought of using in a salad, and also some FAQs about salad prep and increasing salads in your diet.

When greens are what you crave, and vegetables are tasty, salads taste great and Eating Green is exciting!

INGREDIENTS AND TIPS

When I choose what ingredients I will use in a given recipe, I evaluate what will be the most flavorful, provide the most nutrients, and be the most convenient. I feel like if a recipe isn't flavorful and at least somewhat convenient, it will be hard to get around to making it. Especially when it comes to seasonings and shelf-stable ingredients, I like to have ingredients that can be used in multiple recipes. I don't like having to go out and buy an ingredient for just one recipe or go to several different stores to find an ingredient—and I don't want you to have to either. If an ingredient is included in the list below that is a little hard to find, it is because I think it is worth a little extra effort, and I tell you why.

Generally speaking, items in this list go from easiest to store/longest lasting at the start to most perishable at the end. For the perishable items I provide storage tips.

SEASONINGS

- **Salt**—Any salt will work, but I recommend using sea salt or salts that have some trace mineral content. My favorite salt is RealSalt brand. I like it in part because it is mined in my home state of Utah, but mostly because it is handled gently during production and contains many, many trace minerals. To me, its taste is noticeably less harsh than regular table salt. I try to limit salt in my recipes, preferring to use other ingredients and seasonings to boost flavor. If you are under medical orders to limit your salt intake, I suggest using some of my dressing recipes (starting on page 172) instead of store-bought dressing so you can do what you want to with the salt in the recipe. You can also add vegetables like sea beans or chopped Swiss chard stems to your salads since they have a salty flavor.

- **Black Pepper**—To me there is just no comparison between fresh-ground pepper and pepper than comes pre-ground in a can. I think the flavor is quite different between the two—not just the freshness. Fresh ground pepper can make a huge difference in salads, but can be a pain to measure. Here's a trick you can use for measuring fresh ground pepper: Crease piece of paper down the middle, and then lay it flat. Grind the pepper onto the paper—it will tend to flow toward the groove created by the crease. Pick up the paper and allow the pepper to flow along the groove into your measuring spoon. You will probably only need to do this once for any given recipe—after that you will know about how much you need.
- **Dry granulated onion**—Many of my recipes call for dry, granulated onion. Dry granulated onion can be a little more difficult to find in grocery stores, but I think it is worth a little extra effort to find it for several reasons: 1) It is not as cake-y as powdered onion and is therefore easier to measure and use. 2) It rehydrates in foods much faster than minced or chopped dry onion, so you don't have to wait as long for the flavor to blend. 3) It has something of a "cooked" flavor, so it is an easy way to get onion flavor without onion sharpness and without having to cook it. 4) It is an easy way to get a lot of flavor into almost any dish in a way that even people who don't like onion won't really notice. To find dry granulated onion online, look up "granulated onion." I also use various kinds of fresh onion in my salads and information on them will be in the fresh section below.
- **Garlic**—Many of my recipes call for dry granulated garlic. I like to use it for the same reasons I listed above for onion. Many people who object to the aftertaste that comes with fresh garlic will not recognize dry garlic in a recipe, but will notice that the recipe is more flavorful. Some of my recipes also call for "minced garlic (fridge)." What I mean by this is the type of minced garlic that comes in a jar that you can usually find in the produce section of your grocery store. It will keep well for months or even years in your fridge. It has a little more bite than dry garlic, but is not as strong as fresh minced garlic and is more convenient to use than fresh garlic. If you love fresh garlic, feel free to substitute an equal amount of fresh pressed garlic in recipes that call for minced fridge garlic.
- **Ginger**—In most of the recipes that call for ginger I call for "fresh ginger paste." Here again I mean the kind of jar you can get in the grocery store as described above for garlic. Feel free to substitute an equal amount of fresh grated ginger if you prefer. In a couple of recipes I call for dry ginger powder and that is specified in the recipe.
- **Prepared mustard**—In several recipes throughout the book I call for mustard. You can use any kind of mustard that would fall into the "Grey Poupon" or brown mustard category. I would only substitute yellow American mustard in an emergency since it has a fairly different flavor profile. Mustard adds flavor but also acts as an "emulsifier" for dressing. In other words, if mustard is added to an oil and vinegar dressing, it keeps the oil and vinegar from separating (see page 172).
- **Cayenne pepper**—Cayenne consists of ground hot peppers. It is easy to keep on hand, will keep for years, and because it is granulated, its flavor activates relatively quickly, making it easy to tell if you have enough in your recipe (it doesn't take much!). As a substitute, you can use a dash of Tabasco sauce if that is what you have on hand.
- **Cumin**—Cumin is a spice used most often in Middle Eastern and Tex-Mex cooking. It is critical to the flavor profile of several recipes in this book.
- **Dry leaf basil**—Basil is critical to the flavor of Italian

TAKE-AWAY LESSON

As you flip through the salad recipes, you may notice that each recipe in this section has a dot that looks like this titled "Take-away Lesson." These will point out interesting things about that recipe.

recipes and is a wonderful background flavor in many others. Dry basil has a more intense flavor than fresh basil.

- **Dill weed**—Dill weed is not dill seed. Dill seed is primarily used in situations (like pickles) where the flavor has time to seep into the other ingredients. Dill weed is the dry leaf of the dill plant and has a very delicate flavor that works really well in salads and other vegetable dishes.
- **Dry ground or leaf oregano**—Oregano is used mostly to give an "enchilada" flavor or a "Greek" flavor to recipes. You can use either leaf or ground. If the recipe calls for leaf and you have ground, use about ⅔ of the called for amount.
- **Soy sauce, Aloha Shoyu, or tamari**—Full of flavor, these are all variations of soy sauce. Tamari can be gluten-free. Substitute at will.

OILS, DRESSINGS, AND CHEESES:

I put these in the same category because some oil is critical to your body's absorption of the nutrients in vegetables and greens (see page 157). Oils in a salad can come from a dressing or from oily ingredients like avocado and cheese.

- **Olive Oil**—I get extra virgin olive oil at Costco and store some in my kitchen and some in a cool location until I need it. I go through it fast enough that it stays fresh and tastes good. Over time, oils go rancid, which means they develop flavors that are off or bitter. That matters some when you cook with olive oil, but matters much, much more when you are putting it on a salad. Olive oil for salad has to be fresh and have good flavor. I don't recommend using other oils (except as mentioned in specific recipes) because olive oil has been used for millennia and most scientific studies show that it is generally beneficial if used in reasonable amounts. In recipes like The Best Humus (page 170) where you can taste the olive oil flavor, I use cold-pressed extra virgin olive oil from a specialty grower like Sciabica's or Lucero.
- **Mayonnaise**—Mayo, as most people call it, has the reputation of being high fat, but actually is about half water. When used as part of a dressing, it adds creaminess and may have less fat than a vinaigrette. Mayo contains egg as an emulsifier. If you are trying to avoid eggs, try making my Easy Chia Mayo, page 174.
- **Store-bought dressings**—It's easier to eat a salad if it's convenient, and for that reason I use some specific store-bought dressings including Lighthouse Brand Caesar-Caesar, Olive Garden dressing, and others. You can read more about this on page 173.
- **Avocado**—Avocado is a vegetable (well, technically a fruit), but I include it here because avocado gives a dressing-like richness to a salad. It takes the place of oil in the dressing for Brazilian Heart of Palm Salad (page 49) and several of my recipes call for Guacamole (page 168) as a topping.
- **Parmesan cheese**—Parmesan cheese on a salad makes a huge flavor difference. It has actually more protein than fat but still can play a dressing-like role.
- **Goat cheese**—Chèvre from goat milk, commonly called goat cheese, also has a lot of flavor and acts in some ways like dressing. If you don't want to use goat cheese, you can use soft, high-quality feta (but it won't be quite the same). You could also try using sheep's milk feta. It is becoming more available in the United States and has a mild flavor. For more information see page 181.
- **Toasted sesame oil**—I use this in small amounts as a flavoring in oriental and Middle Eastern dishes. You can find it in the Asian section of your grocery store or online. It can be pricey, but I think it is worth the flavor and convenience. One small bottle often lasts me more than a year. It should be stored in the fridge so that it doesn't go rancid.

VINEGAR, LEMON, AND LIME:

Acidic liquids like vinegar and lemon juice are the most critical part of dressing a salad. The vinegars listed here are the ones I keep on hand and the ones I use in recipes in this section. Their flavor differences and different acidity levels make it worth it to me to keep all of them around. Lemon and lime juice can be purchased bottled, but the flavor and nutritional difference between fresh and bottled is huge. Please see page 6 for easy ways to juice fresh lemons or limes.

- **apple cider vinegar**
- **balsamic vinegar**
- **red wine vinegar**
- **rice vinegar**
- **fresh lemon juice**
- **fresh lime juice**

SWEETENERS:

Oil and vinegar dressings are a little milder when they contain something to make them sweet. I like using agave because it dissolves easily and has a relatively neutral flavor; however, you can substitute any of the other sweeteners on this list. In most recipes where I call for honey or maple syrup I want the flavor they provide, while in recipes that call for agave or sugar I am looking for a neutral flavor.

- **agave**
- **maple syrup**
- **sugar**
- **honey**

SHELF-STABLE SALAD TOPPINGS

Toppings like nuts, seeds, olives, and canned and pickled vegetables add interest to a salad and are easy to keep on hand. Here is a list of ones I call for in my recipes. Notes in the recipes explain more.

- **Nuts:** sliced almonds, roasted cashews, roasted soy nuts or wasabi peas
- **Seeds:** sunflower seeds, pumpkin seeds, hemp hearts
- **Dried fruit:** Craisins
- **Canned vegetables:** pinto beans, black beans, diced green chiles
- **Marinated vegetables:** artichoke hearts, Greek olives (Kalamata), heart of palm, celery salad
- **Grain-based toppings**: croutons, pasta

OTHER VEGETABLES AND FRUITS:

- **Yellow, white, and red onions**—Onions add great crunch and flavor to a salad. Please see my website for a video on easy, no-tears cutting (www.Micheles-GreenSmoothies.com.)
- **Leek**—This member of the onion family is less well known in the United States but has a pleasant mild flavor and is quite easy to use.
- **Green onions**—Green onions keep well for about a week in a bag in the fridge. They can keep up to a month in water in a cup on the counter or in the fridge if you change the water every few days. You can even cut off the green part and put it back in the water and new green part will grow if you can keep it on the counter. I like green onions because they are so mild. When using green onions, I often use the green part raw and the white part lightly cooked. I find it easiest to cut green onions using scissors: snip off any dry parts from the green ends. Snip the green part into ¼-inch pieces, and then use the scissors to cut lengthwise down toward to the root and continue snipping the white part (this will make the white part fall into half circles instead of whole circles). Discard the bottom half inch and root. You can freeze the snipped green onions to use later. Please also see the video on my website.
- **Tomatoes**—Years ago one couldn't get tomatoes in the store that even came close to garden tomatoes. Now it's possible to get Campari brand ones on the vine that are very good and full of flavor. A flavorful tomato can make all the difference in a salad or sandwich, so I think it is worth paying a little more to get good ones. I also tend to think that tomatoes that have more flavor are probably more nutritious. When I can't get Campari tomatoes, I get the little containers of grape tomatoes, which also usually have good flavor. There are a few occasions where I need

tomatoes that aren't very juicy and in those situations I use Roma (on the vine when I can get them). Tomatoes taste better and keep longer if they are stored on the counter. If they are stored in the fridge, they go moldy faster. Tomatoes will keep up to two months on the counter.

- **Red, yellow, and orange bell peppers**—Mini peppers (the kind that come in a bag of a variety of colors in the grocery store) keep better, tend to have better flavor, and can be sliced finer, which can be better for some recipes. For fajitas and grilled vegetables regular large bell peppers work better. I don't call for green peppers in any of my recipes.
- **Whole carrots, matchstick carrots, and baby carrots**—I'm much more likely to eat carrots in salads if they are ready to go, so I frequently buy the matchstick carrots available in a bag at my grocery store. If you prefer, you can buy whole carrots and grate them yourself. These are cheaper and more flavorful. If I want a little bit of carrot in a salad and don't want to grate them, I will use a potato peeler to "cut" thin short pieces for a salad. It's a fast and easy way to get some color into a tossed salad. I don't generally use baby carrots in salads, but I like to eat them as a snack.
- **Cucumber**—I generally prefer long English cucumbers unless I have access to fresh garden-grown ones.
- **Broccoli florets**—it's easier to buy these prepared in a bag, but they seem to be "sweeter" if you cut your own off a head of broccoli. If I only need the florets, I keep the stems to use in a stir-fry (see page 93).
- **Cabbage**—It's not as hard to shred cabbage using a knife as you would think, but if you don't want to do it, you can use coleslaw mix.
- **Broccoli slaw**—Broccoli slaw comes in bags at the grocery store and is very nice in salads. It can generally be used interchangeably with shredded cabbage.
- **Chinese cabbage**—many people are not familiar with Chinese cabbage, but I really enjoy using it in several different kinds of salads because it has a softer texture and milder flavor than regular cabbage. Chinese cabbage is also called Napa cabbage.
- **Sugar snap peas**—Sugar snap peas have become more common, but there are still people who have never tried them and are missing out! These peas have great crunch and work well whole on a veggie tray or cut up in salads. Unlike garden peas, the peas inside the shell of a sugar snap pea are small and have very little flavor. The flavor and crunch of the sugar snap pea is all in the edible pod. In salads and Asian dishes you can use snow peas if you can't get sugar snap peas.
- **Corn**—In season, I like to cut it off the cob. It has excellent flavor that way, as long as it has been freshly picked. Other times of the year I use frozen corn.
- **Apple**
- **Mango or papaya**

FRESH HERBS

Cilantro and parsley can go bad quickly unless you give them a little attention after you bring them home from the store. I have two ways I like to store fresh herbs.

Way #1: Take the twist-tie off the bundle. Remove any stems that are already wilted or brown. Spread the stems apart in the bag. Twist the bag shut, leaving air in the bag. Refrigerate.

Way #2: Remove the twist-tie and any brown or wilted sprigs. Trim the ends with scissors and place them in a glass of filtered water in the fridge (like you would do with cut flowers). Both of these methods can also work well for bundles of Swiss chard and other greens.

Fresh herbs are easiest and cheapest to keep on hand if you grow them yourself. They can be easily grown in a window box on a counter in a sunny location.

- **Fresh basil**
- **Cilantro**
- **Italian parsley**
- **Chives**

GREENS

Baby greens, such as spring greens and baby arugula, generally come in a bag or plastic box. When buying them, look for bags or boxes that don't seem to have a lot of water accumulated. Lettuces like romaine and butter lettuce come as a head and generally keep a long time. See below for storage hints.

- **Arugula**, also called rocket
- **baby spring greens**
- **Romaine**
- **butter lettuce** (also called Boston or Bibb)

GENERAL TIPS FOR USING AND STORING FRESH INGREDIENTS:

- **Prewashed greens including spinach, spring greens, arugula, and mâche:** Leaves that sit in condensed water in the bag or container they come in will go bad faster. To prevent this, store the bag or container upside down when you get it home, and shake the container after you use some to redistribute the moisture. Put a paper towel in the bottom to absorb moisture.
- **Head lettuce including butter lettuce, romaine, and oak leaf**: These can be stored up to a month or longer if you take care of them. A head of lettuce will hold up longer if you take off any twist ties, rinse it occasionally and re-bag it, or put a damp paper towel in the bottom of the container or bag (near the root end of the head).
- **Storing produce in the fridge:** Put more robust vegetables like cabbage and broccoli in the coldest parts of your refrigerator. Keep lettuces in the warmer parts to make sure they don't freeze. Use the most delicate items in the fridge first.

TAKE-AWAY LESSON

You can make this salad by picking up a bag of prepared romaine, a bottle of dressing, and a container of Parmesan. Toss them together and you are done. Delicious salads don't have to be difficult.

michele's easy caesar salad

Whenever I take this salad to a party I have people ask me how I made it and what is in it. One time one of my nieces called me after a family party to get the recipe because her nine-year old daughter wanted to have it served at her birthday party. Everyone loves this and it is so easy to make—whether for yourself or for a crowd.

INGREDIENTS	SMALL BATCH	LARGE BATCH
romaine lettuce	10-oz. bag or 2 heads of hearts of romaine	2 lbs.
apple cider vinegar	2 tsp.	2 Tbsp.
fresh ground pepper	¼–½ tsp.	1 tsp.
Lighthouse brand Caesar-Caesar dressing	⅓ cup or 2½ oz.	1 cup or 8 oz.
shredded Parmesan cheese	¼–⅓ cup	⅔ cup
garlic croutons (optional)	1 cup	2–3 cups or 5–6 oz.
grape tomatoes (optional)	a handful	1 pint
Serves:	1 to 2	4 to 30 (see Tip)

INSTRUCTIONS

1. If using romaine hearts or heads of romaine, rinse with cold water and cut as shown in the diagram and instructions below (page 40).

2. Put all the lettuce in a large bowl (I like to mix the salad in a large bowl, then transfer it to a serving bowl when I'm done).

3. Add the vinegar and pepper and toss. At this point you can store the salad in a tightly covered bowl or sealed bag for up to 24 hours in the refrigerator.

4. Just before you are ready to serve, add the dressing, half the Parmesan cheese, and half the croutons (if using.) Toss until all the lettuce is evenly coated with dressing.

TOP with the remaining Parmesan, croutons, and add the tomatoes. Serve.

TIPS AND VARIATIONS

- This salad doesn't keep at all well once the lettuce is tossed with the dressing. I usually try to make just the amount I think I will use. On a day I'm really hungry for greens and not eating anything else with this salad, I can get through a whole "small batch" myself. The large batch can feed 3–4 hungry adults who are just eating salad, or 25–30 people at a party where it is being served as a side dish.
- For the romaine in this recipe, I usually use hearts of romaine. You can also use prewashed and cut romaine in bags or whole heads of leafy romaine. If using hearts of romaine or whole heads, you can get the best results by washing and cutting the romaine 24 hours in advance as mentioned in the recipe. The lettuce will be crisper the next day, and won't wilt as easily when you add the dressing.
- The real secret of this salad is the dressing. When I was working as a cook I sampled dozens of Caesar dressings to find one that would have broad appeal and great flavor. I settled on the refrigerated Lighthouse brand Caesar-Caesar. Anything else just doesn't make the same salad. If you are making dressing for a really big group, use Rod's Creamy Caesar that comes in one-gallon containers and is also a refrigerated dressing (available from food service suppliers).
- You can also use my Easy Homemade Caesar dressing (page 180). I made it so that it is a little stronger than the store-bought ones so that you don't need quite as much.
- I like to use shredded Parmesan because it looks nicer and generally works better in the salad than the finely ground Parmesan. I don't usually use croutons because I like the recipe better without them, but if you do decide to use them, I recommend Reese or Cardini for Caesar salad brand croutons.
- For a fun variation, keep your hearts of romaine whole and dip them in Caesar dressing. You can also crush up some croutons and mix with Parmesan. Dip your lettuce leaves in the dressing and then in the crouton/cheese mixture.

HOW TO CUT WHOLE HEADS OF ROMAINE

1. Place the lettuce on a cutting board and hold on to the root end.
2. With a sharp knife, cut through the head of lettuce along the length of the head (in essence you are cutting the leaves in half lengthwise, but only the widest part of the leaves—don't cut through the root.)
3. Rotate the head of lettuce a quarter turn and make a similar cut for the other side.
4. Keep holding on to the root. Starting at the tip of the leaves, cut the lettuce in one-inch slices (see diagram). Discard the root end.

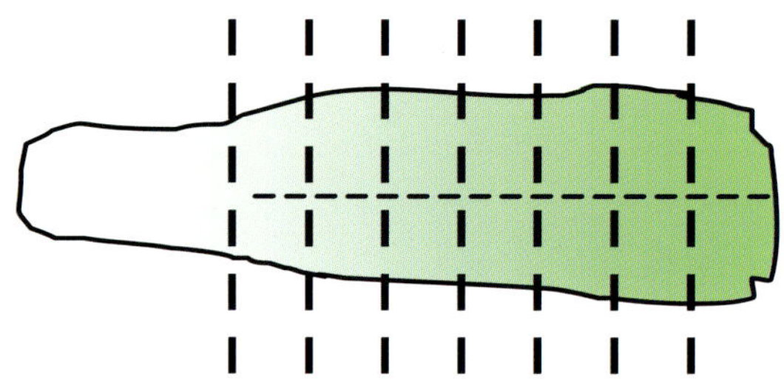

NOTE: It's often said that you shouldn't cut lettuce with a metal knife, but in years of experimenting, I have never had any problem with cutting lettuce this way using a stainless or high-carbon stainless knife.

walt's coleslaw

As long as I can remember, my dad has loved coleslaw. When I was a kid, my mom made a special cooked dressing with vinegar, onion, and sugar that was mixed with mayo after it cooled. Later, my dad started experimenting with mixing his own dressing from existing dressings in the fridge, eventually settling on a combination of Italian dressing and mayo with fresh ground black pepper. This version is just different enough from "normal" coleslaw dressings to make it fun and interesting . . . and it's very popular at family parties, especially alongside fresh garden tomatoes and Betty's Cucumbers.

INGREDIENTS	1X	4X
olive garden dressing or zesty Italian	2 Tbsp.	½ cup
mayo or chia mayo	6 Tbsp.	1½ cups
fresh ground pepper	¼ tsp.	1 tsp.
shredded cabbage	16 oz. (about ½ of a large cabbage)	4 pounds (about 2 large heads)
Serves	4	16 to 20

INSTRUCTIONS

1. Mix the Italian dressing, mayo, and pepper until the dressing is completely smooth. Pour part of the dressing over your cabbage and mix.

2. Add the rest of the dressing, or most of the rest of the dressing, depending on how "saucy" you like your coleslaw. Serve immediately.

TIPS AND VARIATIONS

- This recipe is based on cabbages that weigh around 2½ pounds whole.
- The dressing part of the 1x recipe makes 4 ounces (½ cup) dressing.
- You can add a couple of small diced tomatoes, 20–30 stems of snipped chives or the snipped green part of 4–6 green onions to the 1x recipe.
- If you like your coleslaw dressing a little sweeter, add about a teaspoon of agave to the 1x recipe.
- You can use straight cabbage or cabbage with some chopped kale. One way to do this is to buy a 10-oz. bag of shredded cabbage or a 14-oz. bag of coleslaw mix (cabbage plus carrot) and add 2–6 ounces finely chopped curly kale.
- If you would like to try the cooked coleslaw dressing my mom used to make, here's the recipe: In a small saucepan combine ½ cup sugar and ½ cup apple cider vinegar. Boil together for one minute. Cool slightly, then add a paste made of one teaspoon dry mustard with one teaspoon water. Sprinkle in ½ teaspoon minced dry onion. Store in fridge. Mix with mayo when ready to use.

TAKE-AWAY LESSON

We often equate cabbage with coleslaw, but there are lots of ways to use cabbage for a salad—a simple online search on "cabbage salad" can give you lots of fun options to try!

butter lettuce and tomato salad

This salad only has two ingredients (besides the dressing) and is one of my favorite salads. Butter lettuce is also known as Boston lettuce and has a delightful, mild flavor. It often comes with the root on and when it does, I can keep it up to two months in my fridge (especially if I give it a little water and trim the leaves a few weeks in.) Even when it comes just as a head without the root, I can keep it up to a month. As I mentioned in the ingredient list for this section, tomatoes can keep at least a month on the counter and keep better on the counter than in the fridge. The fact that the two ingredients in this salad keep so well makes it easy to have this salad anytime—but that's not why it's my favorite. I love the flavor, especially with Elaine's Ranch Dressing, page 176. This salad proves the point that simple can be better.

INGREDIENTS	PER PERSON
butter lettuce	5–7 oz.
vine-ripened tomato	2 small or 1 large (6–7 oz.)
lemon wedge (optional)	1–2 wedges
Serves:	1

INSTRUCTIONS

1. Trim the root from the head of lettuce and gently rinse the outer leaves. Leave the lettuce to drain and cut the tomatoes. With small tomatoes, I cut them in quarters and then cut each quarter in half.

2. Pull off the outer leaves from the head of lettuce and pile them on top of each other on a cutting board.

3. Use a knife to cut the leaves in half along the spine, and then in strips. If the lettuce is still damp, use a salad spinner or paper towel to remove excess water. Once the outer leaves are removed and cut, I cut the remainder of the head just like I would a head of romaine (see page 40).

4. Portion out the lettuce for individual salads. Top with tomatoes and drizzle with dressing. Enjoy.

TIPS AN VARIATIONS

- I often keep the outer leaves of a head of butter lettuce to use in my Salad as a Sandwich because they work so well for that. The inside leaves tend to be more curly and crisp, so I use "the heart" of the head in salads like this one.
- For an even easier salad for two, use one (6-oz.) "Butter Bliss" prepackaged salad from Dole with a five-ounce package baby spring greens. Toss together and snip with scissors (to make the lettuce more compact and bite-sized) before serving.
- One trick I use to decrease the amount of dressing and boost the flavor is to squeeze a lemon wedge over the salad and add some fresh ground pepper before I add the dressing.

TAKE-AWAY LESSON

Find a simple-to-prepare salad that you love and start eating more of it, more often. It doesn't matter so much what dressing you use as long as it will help you eat more greens!

TAKE-AWAY LESSON

Not every salad requires a fork. Almost any salad can be eaten in the form of a wrap or sandwich. (See also page 109.)

salad as a sandwich

One of my local grocery stores makes a delicious whole grain ciabatta roll. Even before I started eating green, I loved using these for sandwiches because they held the fillings in so well and didn't go soggy if I put in sliced tomatoes, even hours later. Sandwiches made with these rolls also became popular for sack lunches on trips with my extended family for the same reason. Now that I'm trying to get lots more greens in my diet, I really like these rolls because they can hold so many greens and veggies! With the right roll, lots of greens and the right spreads and toppings, you won't miss the meat and cheese!

PER PERSON YOU NEED:

- 2½ to 3 ounces of butter lettuce or cabbage leaves. Leaves from the outside of the head work best. It's easier to assemble the sandwich if you cut out the main rib or vein out of each leaf.
- 2 ounces of tomato or one small tomato.
- 1½ to 2 tablespoons of my chia mayo (see page 174), or a little olive oil. Can also use mustard.
- Dry granulated onion. Fresh ground pepper if desired.
- Any of the following: alfalfa sprouts, avocado, thinly sliced red onion, thinly sliced cucumber, thinly sliced cooked bacon (nitrite-free).

INSTRUCTIONS

1. Carefully rinse your butter lettuce and put the leaves to drain. If you are in a hurry you can use a salad spinner or spread the leaves on paper towels to dry. If using cabbage leaves, carefully peel off the outer leaves. If using sprouts from the store, rinse them also.

2. Slice the tomato and any other veggies you want to use that need slicing.

3. Cut open your roll and spread it with mayo, then sprinkle each half generously with dry granulated onion. Add some fresh ground pepper if desired. Alternatively you can brush the insides of the roll with olive oil and grill them before adding the fillings.

4. Place the sliced tomatoes, avocado, and any other sliced vegetables you are using on the bread. Open up the container or bag your sandwich will go into, then fold the lettuce and lay in on the sandwich. Put the top on your sandwich and put it straight into your container or bag so it stays together!

TIPS AND VARIATIONS

- I use the outer leaves of a head of butter lettuce or cabbage for sandwiches and keep the inside leaves to cut up for salads.
- If you don't like mayo, use some olive oil as suggested above or a little butter. Even if you have a good ciabatta roll or other sturdy roll, the bread needs a little bit of some kind of oil to keep from going soggy. In this recipe the spread you use acts like a dressing and helps your body absorb the important nutrients in the veggies. (See page 157.)
- The onion powder is important in this recipe because it provides the background zing of flavor usually provided by lunch meat.

betty's marinated cucumbers

My mom, Betty, is a wonderful gardener. For years she grew all her own tomatoes from seed under grow lights in the kitchen before planting them in the garden. Every year she and my dad cared for over a hundred tomato plants, a long row of cucumbers, and lots more. After being out in the garden tending her tomato plants, my mom would often come back into the house with her thumbs literally green from handling the vines. At those moments I knew what it really meant for someone to be a "green thumb." This recipe came down from my dad's side of the family (at least two generations back), but my mom taught me how to make it so, to me, they are Betty's cucumbers. This is a wonderful, simple way to enjoy garden produce and always made me think of simpler times. In my family this dish is served next to other salads or with fresh garden tomatoes.

INGREDIENTS	1X	2X
apple cider vinegar	3 Tbsp.	6 Tbsp. (3 oz.)
agave or sugar	¾ tsp.	1½ tsp.
salt	¼ tsp.	½ tsp.
fresh ground pepper	¼ tsp.	½ tsp.
cucumber	1 English cucumber or 10–12 oz. garden cucumber	2 English cucumbers or 20-24 oz. cucumber
Serves:	2 to 4	4 to 10

INSTRUCTIONS

1. Combine all the ingredients except the cucumber in a 6- to 8-inch round serving dish.
2. Wash and slice the cucumber. If desired, peel the cucumber leaving stripes of green—this makes for a very pretty presentation.
3. Add ½ to ¾ cup cold water (just enough to cover the cukes). You can use a few ice cubes instead of some of the water. Serve immediately or chill for up to two hours before serving.

TAKE-AWAY LESSON

This recipe shows just how simple it can be to make your own dressing. You only have to make this recipe a few times to know it by heart.

easy greek salad

I first made this salad right when I got home after a ten-day trip. The ingredients had all kept just fine in the fridge and became a delicious crispy salad!

INGREDIENTS	1X	2X
butter lettuce	½ head	1–2 heads
heart of romaine	1 head	2 heads
baby red or orange bell pepper	1	2
sweet white or red onion	¼ of an onion or about 2 oz.	½ onion or about 4 oz.
Kalamata olives	6 or 8	12 or 14
artichoke hearts (optional)	8 or 10	16 or 20
goat cheese chevre crumbles (unopened container)	3–4 oz.	6–8 oz.
As main dish salad serves:	2	4 to 5

INSTRUCTIONS

1. Cut the butter lettuce and romaine as shown in the videos on my website (www.MichelesGreenSmoothies.com) or in the diagram on page 40.

2. Arrange the lettuce in individual bowls. Finely slice the bell pepper, onion, and olives. Arrange evenly over the tops of the salads.

3. Garnish each salad with goat cheese and artichoke hearts as desired. Serve with store-bought Greek dressing or use the dressing in the Tips.

TAKE-AWAY LESSON

It's easy to think that keeping salad ingredients on hand can be difficult. This recipe shows that you can make a fairly complex salad from ingredients you can have on hand all the time.

TIPS

- Butter lettuce and romaine both keep a long time because they are on the head. In my fridge they both keep at least a month as long as they don't get pushed to the part of the fridge where they can freeze! The goat cheese I used was an unopened package—that's why it was still good after ten days.
- I like using the baby sweet peppers because I think they are sweeter (and they seem to keep much longer) but you can use part of a regular size bell pepper for this recipe. Since I didn't have Greek dressing on hand when I got back from my trip, I improvised a dressing like this: ½ cup Greek yogurt, ½ teaspoon dry granulated garlic, 2–3 tablespoons lemon juice, about 1 teaspoon olive oil, ⅛ teaspoon agave, ⅛ teaspoon salt and 1 tablespoon water to make it the right consistency. My current favorite store-bought Greek dressing is Kraft Greek Vinaigrette.

brazilian heart of palm salad

This simple and delicious recipe is typical of the type of salads served on a Brazilian-style salad bar. (See also page 135.)

INGREDIENTS	1X	2X
heart of palm	1 (14-oz.) can	2 (14-oz.) cans
avocado, peel and pit removed	2 Haas avocados or 7–8 oz.	4 Haas avocados or 14–16 oz.
sweet white onion	½ onion or about 5 oz.	1 onion or about 10 oz.
fresh lime juice	2–3 Tbsp. or juice of 1–1½ limes	4–6 Tbsp. or juice of 2–3 limes
Serves:	2 to 3	4 to 6

INSTRUCTIONS

1. Open, drain, and rinse the heart of palm. Cut into small bite-size pieces. Prepare your avocado and cut into small bite-size cubes. Dice the onion (see video on my website, www.MichelesGreenSmoothies.com.)

2. Place all the vegetables in a bowl. Pour the lime juice over the top and gently stir to combine. Serve immediately or up to a day later.

TIPS AND VARIATIONS

- Cans of heart of palm can usually be found near the canned and bottled artichoke hearts on the vegetable aisle in your local grocery store.
- This works best with avocados that are just barely ripe. If you have the chance to use a large Florida avocado, it works slightly better than the Haas ones for this recipe.

TAKE-AWAY LESSON

This recipe has a very simple dressing but uses exotic ingredients. Take a look at the list starting on page 76 for more ingredients you may not have thought of using in a salad.

colorful vegetable salad

This salad is typical of chopped vegetable salads served throughout Europe and around the Mediterranean. When we say "salad" in the United States, we most often think of lettuce. This salad has no lettuce, but lots of colorful vegetables and a light, dill vinaigrette.

DRESSING INGREDIENTS	
lemon juice	½ cup
olive oil	6 Tbsp.
agave or sugar	2 tsp.
salt	¾ tsp.
dry granulated onion	2 tsp.
dry dill weed	1 tsp.
Makes:	¾-1 cup dressing

VEGETABLES	
English cucumber	1
roma tomatoes	4
yellow or orange bell pepper	1
Chinese cabbage, finely sliced	about ¼ head
Serves as side dish:	12 to 20

DRESSING INSTRUCTIONS

1. Prepare and measure your lemon juice. Whisk together with the oil and agave or sugar.

2. Add dry ingredients/herbs. Let stand while you prepare the vegetables.

SALAD INSTRUCTIONS

1. Cut the English cucumber in half or quarters lengthwise, then in thin slices crosswise. Quarter and slice the tomatoes. Remove seeds and stem from the pepper and cut into fine strips or small cubes. Weigh the vegetables and add enough Chinese cabbage to make three pounds total vegetables.

2. Combine all the vegetables in a bowl. Toss with the dressing and serve.

TAKE-AWAY LESSON

The dressing for this salad uses the base ingredients typical of many salads—an acid, an oil, and a sweetener—then adds herbs and seasonings for added flavor.

TIPS AND VARIATIONS

- For variety you can also add any or all of the following to the dressing: 1 teaspoon garlic powder, 2 teaspoon s dry parsley, 2 teaspoons dry chives, ¼ teaspoon ground cumin, ½ teaspoon prepared mustard (like Grey Poupon).
- You can change the vegetables you use—just try to end up with about 3 pounds total prepared vegetables (1 pound vegetables per ~¼ cup dressing).

If you want to make a smaller salad, prepare fewer vegetables and just use as much dressing as you need. Refrigerate the remainder of the dressing to use another time.

- In Germany this type of salad is often served with optional canned corn and flake canned tuna to put over the top and slices of fresh baguette on the side.
- If I'm taking this salad to a party, I usually keep the dressing separate and mix it with the vegetables just before serving. Because there is salt in the dressing, the vegetables will start to "weep" if the dressing is added sooner, effectively thinning the dressing and making it too weak.

arugula salad

This has become one of my favorite salads. In fact, it's one that my husband and I can eat several times a week because it has a "beefy" and hearty feel to it. The first time I tried arugula, I didn't love it. It was a little too sharp and bitter for me. What I didn't know then is that arugula (also called "rocket") needs certain ingredients with it. With the right dressing and ingredients, arugula tastes nutty and simply delicious.

INGREDIENTS	1X	2X
olive oil	2 Tbsp.	¼ cup
vinegar—part balsamic, part apple cider	1½ Tbsp.	3 Tbsp.
agave	2 Tbsp.	¼ cup
baby arugula or young rocket	6 oz.	12 oz.
red onion, finely chopped	1½ oz.	3 oz.
toasted cashews, finely chopped	1 oz. or about ¼ cup	2 oz. or about ½ cup
craisins, chopped	1 oz. or about ¼ cup	2–3 oz. or ½–¾ cup
goat cheese chevre crumbles	3 oz.	6 oz.
As main dish salad serves:	2 to 3	4 to 5

INSTRUCTIONS

1. Measure the liquid ingredients into a small bottle with a lid and shake together.

2. Assemble the other ingredients except the goat cheese in a large salad bowl. The onions can be finely sliced or chopped very small. The craisins work better if they are chopped finer than how they generally come.

3. Just before serving pour the dressing over the salad. Add two-thirds of the goat cheese and toss. Sprinkle the remaining goat cheese over the top. Serve immediately.

TAKE-AWAY LESSON

The dressing for this salad has the same classic dressing components as Colorful Vegetable Salad, but instead of herbs uses flavorful ingredients like onion, goat cheese, and craisins.

TIPS AND VARIATIONS

- Instead of the craisins use sliced fresh strawberries. You will need twice the weight of strawberries as the weight of craisins called for.
- You can buy raw cashews and toast them for this recipe by spreading them on a tray and baking them at 350 degrees until they start to brown. Keep an eye on them because the smaller pieces can quickly go from brown to black. If you prefer you can use roasted salted cashews.

TAKE-AWAY LESSON

The dressing for this salad is based on the most basic form of French vinaigrette: oil, vinegar, and mustard. This version also has some sweetener to make it milder.

crispy pear and belgian endive salad

In the book French Kids Eat Everything, *Karen Le Billon explains that it is easier for kids and adults to get used to a new fruit or vegetable if the new item is served with something more familiar. In this simple recipe, crispy pears (something familiar) are served with crispy Belgian endive (something much less familiar.) Tiny heads of Belgian endive look a little bit like miniature heads of Romaine. They have great crunch and mild flavor. This salad was inspired by something I ate at Provisions Restaurant, a creation of Chef Tyler Stokes. For variety, I'm presenting this salad as a finger salad. It's a fun way to explore the new flavors!*

INGREDIENTS
crispy pear; core removed and cut into thin slices
Belgian endive; washed and trimmed so that the leaves separate
One recipe of classic Vinaigrette
Raw walnuts and small cubes of blue cheese (optional)

CLASSIC FRENCH VINAIGRETTE

INGREDIENTS	1X	4X
olive oil	¼ cup.	1 cup
red wine vinegar	1½ Tbsp.	6 Tbsp.
agave	1¼–1½ tsp.	1½–2 Tbsp.
Dijon-style mustard	1 tsp.	4 tsp.
Makes:	~⅓ cup	1⅓ cup

INSTRUCTIONS

1. Give each person an individual dipping cup of dressing. Arrange the pears and endive on a serving tray. Add bowls of walnuts and blue cheese if desired.

2. Everyone takes pieces of pear or endive to dip. Alternate with eating walnuts and cheese if desired.

TIPS AND VARIATIONS

- You can present this salad as a normal "fork" salad—simply cut the pear and endive leaves in bite size pieces and toss with just enough of the dressing to coat. Add some raw chopped walnuts and a few crumbles of high quality blue cheese.
- I'm not normally a huge fan of eating blue cheese straight, but I recently tasted one that was so yummy I wanted to gobble it up! The cheese is made by Rogue Creamery in Oregon and is called "Caveman Blue." Rogue Creamery cheeses are available in most states. Their website is www.RogueCreamery.com.

classic broccoli salad

When I was working as a cook at a girls camp I tried to make foods that the campers (who were only there for a week) would like, but also keep the staff happy (who were there all summer.) When I introduced a salad bar, the most popular item with the staff was a broccoli salad similar to this one.

INGREDIENTS	1X	4X
mayonnaise	¼ cup	1 cup
vinegar—red wine or cider	2 Tbsp.	½ cup
agave	3 Tbsp.	¾ cup
craisins	½ cup, about 2 oz.	2 cups, about 8 oz.
toasted cashews	¼–½ cup, 1–2 oz.	1–2 cups, about 4–8 oz.
sunflower or pumpkin seeds	¼ cup, about 1 ounce	1 cup, about 4 oz.
thinly sliced red onion	2 oz.	8 oz.
broccoli florets	10 oz., about 4 cups	2½ lbs
As main dish salad, serves:	2	8

INSTRUCTIONS

1. Make the dressing by combining the mayo, vinegar, and agave.
2. Measure the craisins, nuts, seeds, and finely sliced red onion into a large mixing bowl. Mix in the dressing.
3. Wash and prepare the broccoli. Add it to the bowl and stir until the broccoli is evenly coated with dressing.
4. Salad can be eaten immediately but tastes even better 8, 24, or 48 hours later.

TAKE-AWAY LESSON

This salad is of a type that actually improves with time. As the broccoli sits in the acidic dressing, it becomes softer and more easily digestible—similar to what would happen if you lightly cooked it.

TIPS

- You can make this salad healthier by using my Chia Mayo (page 174) for the dressing and toasting your own cashews. You can toast cashews by spreading them on a baking sheet and baking them at 350 degrees until they start to brown. Keep an eye on them as they can quickly go from brown to burned.
- The smaller the florets are, the better this salad comes across. The easiest way to get tiny florets is to cut off the stems. You can chop the stems and use them in the salad or save them to use in a stir-fry. (See page 93).
- While this salad is plenty flavorful without it, bacon adds a nice smoky flavor. If you want to add crispy crumbled bacon to this recipe, I suggest using nitrite-free bacon, available in your local health food store and at some grocery stores.
- This is a great salad to take to a party or pot luck.

TAKE-AWAY LESSON

This salad and the next two are part of a category I call "dense salads that can go on top of greens." With this vegetable-heavy pasta salad, you can mix greens into the pasta salad, serve it on top of greens, or both.

greek pasta salad

INGREDIENTS	1X	2X
cooked pasta—your choice	4 oz.	8 oz.
Greek dressing	¼–⅓ cup	½–⅔ cups
yellow or orange pepper	about half of a bell pepper	about 1 whole bell pepper
cucumber	about a quarter of an English cucumber (2–3 oz.)	about half of an English cucumber (5–6 oz.)
diced tomatoes	6–8 oz.	12–16 oz.
red onion, finely sliced	1 oz.	2 oz.
Greek olives (Kalamata), sliced	1 oz.	2 oz.
crumbled goat cheese or feta	2 oz.	4 oz.
fresh basil leaves	8–10 leaves	16–20 leaves
baby arugula/rocket	2–3 oz.	4–6 oz.
Makes:	5–6 cups	10–16 cups

INSTRUCTIONS

1. Cook pasta. Drain and rinse with cold water. Toss with Greek dressing and refrigerate overnight.

2. Add diced pepper, cucumber, tomatoes, sliced red onion, and olives. Stir.

3. Just before serving, prepare basil and arugula. To prepare the basil, pile up the leaves, roll them together tightly, and cut crosswise with scissors to make narrow strips. Place the arugula in a bowl and use scissors to cut it into smaller pieces. Stir both gently into the pasta salad along with the goat cheese or feta.

TIPS

- You can use any gluten-free, whole grain, or other pasta. I like using multicolored pasta.
- The technique I describe for cutting the basil in this recipe is called *chiffonade*. You can look it up online to learn more about it.
- To boost the greens content even more, you can serve this salad on a bed of spring greens drizzled with Greek dressing.
- My current favorite store-bought Greek dressing is Kraft Greek Vinaigrette.

asian crunch salad

My local grocery store deli sells a salad similar to this one that I like to get on busy days to have for dinner or take for lunch. This recipe is almost as easy as buying it. For dinner I usually serve it on top of a bed of greens drizzled with a spicy Asian dressing.

INGREDIENTS	1X	2X
rice vinegar	2 Tbsp.	¼ cup
sesame oil	2–3 Tbsp.	4–6 Tbsp.
agave	1 Tbsp.	2 Tbsp.
soy sauce	1½ tsp.	3 tsp.
green onions	½–¾ oz. (¼-⅓ cup snipped)	1-1½ oz. (½-⅔ cup snipped)
sliced almonds	1–2 oz. (½ cup)	2–4 oz. (1 cup)
sunflower seeds (can also use sesame)	1 oz.	2 oz.
roasted salted soy nuts (can also used roasted edamame, wasabi peas,chopped cashews or peanuts)	¼ cup	½ cup
fresh sugar snap or snow peas	2 oz.(about 10 pods)	4 oz. (about 20 pods)
broccoli slaw	6 oz. (½ pkg.)	12 oz. (1 pkg.)
Makes:	4 cups	8 cups
As main dish salad, serves:	1 to 2	3 to 4

INSTRUCTIONS

1. Whisk together the vinegar, oil, agave, and soy sauce in a large bowl.

2. Use scissors to finely snip the green onion. Place these in the mixing bowl with the dressing along with all the nuts and seeds called for. Stir.

3. Use scissors to snip the peas into bite-size pieces. Add the peas and broccoli slaw to the bowl and mix.

4. Marinate at least 30 minutes before serving. Tastes best after 2–3 days of marinating in the refrigerator.

SERVING SUGGESTION: For two salads, prepare two bowls, each with about five ounces baby mixed greens, Romaine, or other greens. Drizzle with Asian dressing (use the recipe on page 73 or Trader Joe's Spicy Asian Vinaigrette). Top each salad with 1½ to 2 cups of Asian Crunch Salad.

TIPS AND VARIATIONS

- Instead of the last nuts, you can use diced teriyaki chicken or diced breaded spicy chicken fingers. For 1x batch use 2 ounces (about one chicken strip).
- You can use an equal weight of shredded cabbage instead of broccoli slaw.
- If eating this salad right away, you may want to leave out the soy nuts.

TAKE-AWAY LESSON

The important thing in this salad is the texture. The salad keeps for three days (or longer) and the different ingredients will have different textures on day one, day two, and day three.

black bean and corn salad

This has become one of my favorite salads to serve when we have guests, especially in the summer when corn on the cob and tomatoes are at their best. It is an easy salad to throw together and everyone likes it. You can serve it as a dip with chips or over greens drizzled with my creamy Cilantro-Lime Dressing (see page 178).

INGREDIENTS	1X	2X
16-oz. can of black beans	½ can	1 can
fresh tomatoes, diced	8 oz.	16 oz.
fresh corn cut off the cob or frozen corn	1 cob or about ¾ cup	2 cobs or about 1½ cups
sweet red or white onion, finely chopped	2 oz.	4 oz.
fresh cilantro	about ¼ bunch or as desired	about ½ bunch or as desired
fresh lime juice	2 Tbsp.	¼ cup
dry ground cumin	¼ tsp.	½ tsp.
dry granulated onion	¼ tsp.	½ tsp.
cayenne pepper	a dash	a dash or two
hemp hearts (optional)	2 Tbsp.	¼ cup
4-oz. can diced green chiles (optional)	½ can	1 can
Over greens with guacamole serves:	2 to 3	4 to 6

INSTRUCTIONS

1. Drain and rinse the beans. Dice the tomatoes, cut the corn off the cob and finely chop the onion. Gently mix them together in a serving bowl.

2. Wash and dry the cilantro and use scissors to finely snip it. Add the cilantro, lime juice, cumin, dry onion, cayenne pepper, and hemp hearts to the bowl. Add the diced green chiles if desired. Gently mix.

3. Serve over greens drizzled with your choice of southwest dressing. Top with my guacamole (see page 168) and serve with tortilla chips.

TIPS

- In this recipe the hemp hearts and diced green chiles are optional, but I think it tastes best with them. Hemp hearts are a nutritious seed that can be found in many grocery stores as well as health food stores.
- Be cautious with the cayenne pepper—a single dash can add quite a bit of heat. It takes a little time for the cayenne to rehydrate in the salad, so it's best to wait about ten minutes after you add the cayenne before deciding if you need more.
- You can also do this salad as a wrap: Spread some guacamole down the middle of a large tortilla. Layer greens over the guac and add the bean and corn salad down the middle over the greens. Roll, cut in half, and package up for a great take-with-you lunch.

TAKE-AWAY LESSON

Because this salad can be eaten so many ways and is so appealing, it's a good salad for introducing people to the idea that it is possible to really be full and satisfied just eating salad.

TAKE-AWAY LESSON

Doing your own salad bar doesn't have to be complicated. You just need greens and vegetables that are really fresh and have a variety of textures and colors.

party salad tray

I had the chance to attend the fiftieth wedding anniversary celebration of the parents of some of my good friends in Germany. The food was delicious and the presentation was simple but elegant. One of the things that impressed me was this gorgeous salad tray. It served the same purpose as a salad bar, allowing each guest to make their own salad, but was so much simpler . . . and at the same time so very pretty! Even after guests started taking some, it still looked nice.

SOME SUGGESTED INGREDIENTS	
red or green frisee (see page 77)	sliced radishes
baby arugula	sliced peppers of various colors
grated carrot	shaved fresh fennel (see page 76)
sliced tomato	micro greens (see page 77)
sliced cucumber	edible flowers (see page 78)
finely shaved or sliced red onion	butter lettuce, torn in pieces
grated or spiralized jicama (see page 77 and page 134)	romaine lettuce, finely sliced

TIPS AND VARIATIONS

- When talking about eating nutritiously, one favorite phrase is to "eat a rainbow." It's something to keep in mind in selecting vegetables for a tray like this—different colors make it look and taste delicious!
- The next two recipes in this section can be presented as a salad bar. You can use this Party Salad Tray idea to make it simpler and easier to serve Roots Café Chop Salad or Kristi's Vietnamese Salad for a group.
- See my website (www.MichelesGreenSmoothies.com) for more ideas.

roots café chop salad

A few months ago I discovered a wonderful cafe, located just a few blocks from where I live. For the first couple months after I found it, my husband and I ate there almost every week, excited to try all the healthy, high-quality and tasty menu items they had. Co-owner Wendy Phelps says, "Bill and I opened Roots Café with the intention of inspiring our guests to be more conscious of the foods they choose to eat. We also wanted a great place for those with special dietary needs to be able to come and find some good health and flavorful options. We make all items from real food, some local, some organic, but all fresh!" What I love about Roots Cafe is that the emphasis is on enjoying the really wonderful flavors that can come from truly fresh homemade food. I feel privileged to include their house salad in this book and also excited because it is a "chopped salad." A chopped salad is basically just a green salad with toppings, but everything is chopped fine (including the lettuce) and tossed together with the dressing. Wendy and Bill say: "This salad can literally have all your favorite salad items in it. The key is to keep the texture and tartness balanced. So feel free to toss out what you may not like and add things that you do. There are not measurements; just use how much you'd like. Kind of like when you're at a salad bar . . ."

INGREDIENTS	
romaine lettuce, very finely chopped	celery, finely diced
red leaf lettuce, very finely chopped	artichoke hearts, cut into small pieces
frisee lettuce, finely chopped or cut fine with scissors	capers (see Tips below)
baby spinach, finely chopped or cut fine with scissors	Stilton Blue Cheese, crumbled or in small cubes
orange bell pepper (or small baby bell pepper), finely diced	dry salami, finely sliced and cut into quarters (optional)
red onion, very finely diced	lemon basil dressing, recipe on next page

INSTRUCTIONS

1. Prepare the amount of vegetables, lettuce and toppings you think you want in your salad. (At Roots, they use 10–12 oz.) If you are doing this for a group, you can set out the ingredients, let each person put the amount of each ingredient they want into a bowl, and then toss each person's salad with the dressing.

2. Transfer the salad once it is mixed to a plate and enjoy!

TIPS

- Capers are the small, mildly spicy flower buds of the caper plant, preserved in vinegar. In a salad they add wonderful small bursts of flavor, but are best used sparingly. They come in small jars and are usually located near the artichoke hearts in your grocery store.
- At Roots Cafe, they serve the chop salad on chilled plates. This keeps the salad crisp and tasty while you eat it.

TAKE-AWAY LESSON

A chopped salad is one way to have a really dense, filling salad that still has a lot of greens.

ROOTS CAFÉ LEMON BASIL DRESSING

INGREDIENTS	1X	2X
sour cream	1 cup	2 cups
fresh lemon juice	3 Tbsp.	6 Tbsp.
lemon zest	from ½ lemon	from 1 lemon
chopped fresh basil leaves	about ¼ cup	about ½ cup
Makes:	about 6 oz.	about 12 oz.

INSTRUCTIONS

1. Combine the ingredients in a blender and purée. (Can use Greek yogurt instead of sour cream if desired.)

2. Mix in some dry granulated garlic and fresh ground pepper as desired. (You can also add salt, but probably don't need any if you add the salty items such as capers, blue cheese, and salami to your salad.)

kristi's vietnamese salad

Most of my family like experimenting with food and tweaking recipes. My niece Kristi is no exception. She loves trying out healthy recipes and is always trying out new salads she can take to work for lunch. One Saturday that was busy day for me she brought me this delicious salad packed in a plastic container as a single serving. I loved the blend of flavors and textures and especially the fresh flavor from the herbs.

Like the Roots Café Chop Salad, this is a salad where you can choose your ingredients like at a salad bar. You can make it for a single meal, package up enough for two days of lunches or serve it as a salad bar for a group.

INGREDIENTS	
romaine lettuce, very finely chopped	fresh mint leaves, chopped
carrots, finely grated, matchstick or shaved (see Tip below)	fine rice noodles (optional)
red or yellow bell pepper (mini ones preferred), finely sliced	roasted peanuts, chopped (optional)
cucumber, sliced in long thin strips and then chopped	cooked chicken tenders, finely diced (optional)
celery, sliced in long, very thin strips and then chopped (optional)	frozen cooked shrimp, thawed (optional)
cilantro, chopped	spicy Asian dressing of your choice—see Tips
fresh basil leaves, chopped	

INSTRUCTIONS

1. If using fine rice noodles, soak them to soften (follow package directions.) Prepare all your vegetables and herbs. The herbs are critical to the flavor of this salad.

2. Assemble the salad. Like with the Roots Cafe Chop Salad you can choose your own amounts and ingredients.

3. If eating the salad later, put your ingredients in a sealed container and refrigerate—the salad will keep great for about 24 hours. When ready to eat, drizzle with dressing and enjoy.

TIPS AND VARIATIONS

- An easy way to make a few shaved carrots for this salad is to do it with a potato peeler. I use the peeler to quickly shave off short pieces of carrots into the salad. It is easy and fast and looks pretty.
- You can use the peanut variation of the dressing for my Seared Ahi Salad for this salad. I also recommend Trader Joe's Spicy Asian Vinaigrette. Because of the herbs in the salad you may not need as much dressing as you would normally expect to use.

- A really fun way to serve this salad is as a Vietnamese-style fresh spring roll. All you have to do is get the rice wrappers, briefly dip them in water, and use them to wrap the yummy, fresh ingredients. You can find tutorials by looking up "Vietnamese spring roll" online. If serving the salad this way, leave the cucumbers and celery in long, very thin strips (like a carrot stick but much smaller diameter).

TAKE-AWAY LESSON

Fresh herbs mixed in with the greens can give your salad a bright, fresh flavor.

european layered salad

While there are layered salad recipes popular here in the United States, this recipe is typical in Germany—and one that you will find some version of at nearly every pot-luck event. This salad can also be served as a "Salad Torte." Details on how to do this are below.

INGREDIENTS	
romaine, thinly sliced	about 2 hearts of romaine
ground black pepper	about ¼ tsp.
apple, finely diced	½–1 apple
frozen corn	6–8 oz.
"celery salad" (see Tip)	12-oz. jar
finely sliced leek	1 leek
mayonnaise or chia mayo	enough to cover the top of the salad
Pan size:	9 x 13 Pyrex
Serves as a side dish:	12 to 15

INSTRUCTIONS

1. Wash and finely slice the romaine (see instructions, page 42.) Cut enough romaine to fill a 9×13 glass baking dish or pan about ¾ full (the lettuce will compress some as you add the toppings.)

2. Grind black pepper over the surface of the lettuce or sprinkle evenly with pepper. Turn the lettuce over or toss it a little to distribute the pepper.

3. Finely dice the apple and distribute evenly over the surface of the salad. Distribute the corn evenly over the apple. Thoroughly drain the celery salad and distribute it over the corn.

4. Slice the leek once the long way and thoroughly wash each half, letting water run through the layers. Finely slice both halves starting from the green end and working toward the root. Discard the root. Sprinkle the white parts of the leek over the salad and some of the green parts. Keep some to use as a garnish.

TAKE-AWAY LESSON

This salad can be made ahead and is perfect for taking to a party. Taking a fun salad to a party insures you will have something green to eat while you are there

Pictured here: Salad Torte Variation (see page 72).

5. Spread mayonnaise over the top of the salad. I like to do this by using a very small cookie scoop and putting small scoops of mayo at even intervals over the top, then spreading them to make an even layer, almost like frosting a cake.

6. Garnish with some green leek and a few sprinkles of sweet ground paprika if desired. Store in the refrigerator for 12 to 24 hours before serving. Serve in sections, like serving a cake, so that each serving has some of each layer.

TIPS

- The ingredients aren't as exact for this salad because you can play with the amounts. You just want to end up with a good balance of greens to toppings and not too thick a layer of dressing over the top.
- In the finished salad, you can't really taste the black pepper. When black pepper sits for a few hours or a day with lettuce, it improves the lettuce flavor in a subtle way, but doesn't have a strong presence of its own.
- Even though the mayo has no seasonings added, flavors from the vegetables, the black pepper, and the apple will delicately flavor it as it sits and make it taste like a flavored dressing. People will ask you what's in it and be surprised when you say "nothing." Because the dressing isn't touching most of the lettuce—just the toppings—the lettuce doesn't wilt or weep. If desired, you can mix the mayo with some Greek yogurt or sour cream before you put it on the salad.
- "Celery salad" is matchstick celery root bottled in a light vinegar marinade. It is available in some grocery stores and you can also find it on Amazon. It is the most typical ingredient in salads of this type in Germany. If you prefer, you can try using some grated fresh celery root.
- This recipe works best in a pan like a 9×13 cake pan. You can do it in a glass bowl or trifle dish and it looks really pretty, but it is harder to get part of each layer with each scoop of salad.
- You can make individual portions of this salad to take for lunches. They should keep about three days.

VARIATIONS

- **Salad Torte:** Line a springform pan with plastic wrap. Instead of sliced romaine hearts, use the top half of the outer leaves of green leafy romaine, outer leaves of butter lettuce, or baby spring greens. Layer these, keeping them as flat as possible and filling out to the edges and making sure all the space is evenly filled. Add the toppings in layers as directed above. Spread the dressing over the top and add pretty garnishes to make it look like a decorated "cake." (For ideas, do an image search on "Salat Torte"—German for Salad Torte.) When ready to serve, remove the sides of the springform pan, fold the plastic wrap under the base, and place on a round serving tray. Cut in wedges with a sharp knife and serve with a cake server.
- **Layered Taco Salad:** Prepare lettuce as directed above. For toppings use diced roma tomatoes, green onion, drained and rinsed pinto beans, and sliced avocado. For the dressing, mix sour cream or Greek yogurt with taco seasoning. Garnish with green onion or finely sliced red pepper. Offer salsa and chips on the side when serving.
- **Classic Garden Salad:** Prepare lettuce as directed above. For toppings use quartered and sliced tomatoes, diced cucumber, finely sliced red onion, finely sliced radish, or grated carrot. Garnish with snipped parsley or chives. Can use bacon bits or diced hard-boiled egg in the salad or on top as a garnish.
- **Shrimp Salad:** Prepare lettuce as above. For toppings use finely diced dill pickles (can be finely chopped in a food processor), salad shrimp, and diced apple or finely diced sweet onion. Squeeze a little lemon juice over this and top with mayo. Garnish with fresh dill snipped into small pieces. For a last-minute salad or for a salad to serve one, mix these toppings with mayo and serve on a bed of lettuce with a sprig of fresh dill. This is based on a traditional northern German salad recipe.

seared ahi salad

I never thought seared ahi was something I would enjoy. First off, it's tuna and I associated tuna with lunchroom sandwiches. Second, it tended to be served a little too much on the rare side for my taste. I didn't know that seared ahi, when it is really fresh, has no fishy flavor at all and has a very smooth, non-offensive texture. When I had it the first time, served on a salad similar to this one in Hawaii, I realized what I had been missing.

SALAD INGREDIENTS	PER PERSON
Chinese cabbage	5–6 oz.
sweet white onion	1–2 oz.
Haas avocado	¼ avocado (~1½ oz.)
ripe mango	¼ mango
small Hawaiian papaya (optional)	¼ papaya
fresh wild ahi tuna	3 oz.
Feeds:	1

ASIAN DRESSING INGREDIENTS	1X	2X
Soy sauce	3 Tbsp.	6 Tbsp. (3 oz)
toasted sesame oil	1 Tbsp.	2 Tbsp.
crushed ginger (fridge)	2–3 tsp.	1½–2 Tbsp.
honey	1 Tbsp.	2 Tbsp. (1 oz)
Dijon or similar mustard	1 Tbsp.	2 Tbsp. (1 oz)
dry granulated garlic	¼ tsp.	½ tsp.
dry granulated onion	¼ tsp.	½ tsp.
sesame oil or sesame oil blend	½ cup	1 cup
Makes:	6 oz.	12 oz.

INSTRUCTIONS

1. Measure all the dressing ingredients except the sesame oil/sesame oil blend into a small serving pitcher and whisk to combine. Add the sesame oil and whisk again until well blended.

2. Prepare individual bowls of salad: slice the chinese cabbage and onion and spread evenly in the bottom of the bowl. Peel and cut slices off the mango. Peel the papaya, cut it in quarters, and remove the seeds. Cut the avocado in quarters, remove the pit, and remove the peel. Cut the avocado and papaya quarters into slices and arrange them on the salad(s). Do the same with the mango slices.

3. Set the salad(s) aside and get out the ahi. Pour some of the dressing into a shallow bowl to use as a marinade on the ahi. You will need one tablespoon of marinade for every three ounces of ahi you are using. Dip the ahi in the marinade, turning it to coat all sides.

TAKE-AWAY LESSON

Many typical American salads are loaded with cheddar cheese or large amounts of chicken. This salad shows how just a little bit of fresh, high-quality meat can make a salad special and delicious.

4. Preheat a sauté pan over high heat. When the pan is hot, quickly sear all sides of the tuna, using tongs to turn it and support it so that the sides can also be seared. When all the sides are lightly seared, lay the ahi in the pan and allow the bottom to brown slightly. Turn and brown the other side. This whole cooking process should take no more than three minutes total.

5. Remove the ahi from the pan and allow it to stand for about five minutes before slicing (this will help it retain its moisture when you cut it).

DRIZZLE the salad(s) with a little dressing. Thinly slice the ahi and lay the pieces on the salad (or salads). Drizzle with more dressing and serve immediately.

FOOD SAFETY TIPS

- Choose ahi that looks bright red and fresh and has no fishy smell.
- Pick up the fish right before you leave the store.
- Pack it next to frozen items or on an ice pack for transporting home in hot weather.
- Use it the day you buy it and try not to have leftovers.
- See also FAQs on page 79.

TIPS AND VARIATIONS

- Seared ahi doesn't reheat well and isn't as good served cold either, so I try to buy just the amount I will need when I make the salad. Good ahi can be expensive, but you don't need much to make this delicious salad. With current pricing and the amount I use per person, the ahi would cost between two and a half and three dollars per person. Ahi is also known as yellowfin tuna.
- This recipe works best with avocados that are on the less-ripe side.
- Small Hawaiian papayas are easier to cut and use than the large Mexican ones and have a pleasant flavor as long as they are not overripe. In picking one out, don't look at the color of the skin (ranges from green to yellow) but rather check for ripeness by holding them. A ripe papaya will "give" slightly like a ripe peach or nectarine. An overripe one will feel soft and an underripe one will feel hard. The round, black seeds of the papaya are edible. They are soft but crunchy and have a slightly "peppery" taste like watercress. I like to use them as a garnish when I make this salad.
- You can use this dressing recipe for other Asian salads. For a slight variation, use peanut butter instead of mustard.

USING UNUSUAL VEGETABLES, FRUITS, AND GREENS IN SALADS

There are lots of good vegetables, greens, and even fruits that can be used in salads that most people in the United States aren't too familiar with. Below is a list of produce you might want to try out at some point to add variety to your salads. Some of the vegetables will reappear in other dishes later in this book.

- **Asparagus**—Asparagus can be eaten raw or cooked. Raw, it has a nice crunch, but a strong flavor. Asparagus that is lightly cooked and cut in pieces can be wonderful in a salad. In a salad I would serve it over butter lettuce with a creamy honey-mustard dressing and a sprinkle of Parmesan cheese.
- **Artichoke hearts**—Although these are relatively well-known (and appear in some of my recipes), I wanted them on this list as a reminder. Available bottled, in water, in an oil marinade, or frozen, artichoke hearts can add flavor and flair to many dishes. Artichoke hearts canned in water tend to be a little less tender than those canned in marinade.
- **Beet**—Most people aren't aware that beet can be eaten raw. It has mild flavor, good crunch, and, finely shredded or spiralized, it adds great color.
- **Belgian endive** (see photo)—This little known salad green looks like a very small head of romaine. The leaves have great crunch, are generally mild, and are a good size for dipping. I have seen the leaves used whole around a salad or salad platter to make it prettier and add variety. Individual leaves would work well as part of a veggie tray with dip.
- **Celery root** (see photo)—This root vegetable has long been popular in Europe but still is relatively unknown in the United States. I really like it because its flavor is milder than stock celery and it has a creamy texture. Eaten raw it has a nutty flavor and a mild aroma only vaguely reminiscent of celery. To use it, cut off the bumpy exterior to expose the creamy white interior. Grate it to use raw or finely dice and sauté—either way it can add a different dimension to a salad. It is said that Mary, Queen of Scots, enjoyed a salad made from diced cooked celery root tossed with lettuce, creamy mustard dressing, Italian parsley, and hard-cooked egg slices. Sounds pretty good to me! See pages 104 and 162 for recipes later in the book that use celery root.

- **Chayote** (see photo)—Chayote is little known in the United States but is used extensively in Mexico and South America. It is related to summer squash and cucumber and has a texture somewhere between the two. It has a very mild flavor similar to cucumber. Try it sometime diced or sliced in any salad.
- **Fennel (see photo)**—While fennel can refer to an aromatic seed, here I'm referring to the bulbous stock vegetable that looks a little like celery. When cut, it has a strong anise (licorice) aroma. Like celery root, it can be used raw or cooked. A delicious salad I had at a restaurant once had mixed greens, cinnamon walnuts, goat cheese crumbles, red onion, a light vinaigrette, and thin shaved fennel. If you weren't looking for the fennel as you ate the salad, you wouldn't notice it, but it definitely added crunch and enhanced the overall flavor profile. It also goes well with crispy pear.

- **Fig**—I have had salads with fresh fig, cut in quarters, and also dried fig, cut in small pieces. I've never loved Fig Newtons, but find fig in salad very tasty!
- **Frisée** (see photo)—Frisée's main attraction is that it is so pretty. If you are looking for greens that will make a salad or salad tray look more exciting or intriguing, frisée is the lettuce to go for.
- **Green garbanzo beans or soaked garbanzo beans**—Green garbanzo beans are sometimes sold at regular grocery stores. They look and taste similar to peas in a pod. Soaked dry garbanzo beans, while being yellow instead of green, have a similar taste and great crunch (see page 164). Try chopping the garbanzo beans roughly and using them on top of a tossed salad or in a salad like my Asian Crunch Salad.
- **Herbs**—Not that we don't all know about herbs, but we don't always think to put fresh herbs in a salad. Fresh cilantro tastes great tossed into an Asian salad, fresh snipped basil in an Italian salad. Fresh snipped chives in any garden salad. The green ends of fresh green onion go well in any Asian salad and in almost any other salad.
- **Jicama** (see photo)—Pronounced "hick-a-muh," this vegetable has wonderful crunch and very mild flavor. It's one of my very favorite fresh veggies to have on a veggie tray or eat with my Salad as a Sandwich. In the United States, some people eat it often while others have never had it. If you are one of those who have never tried it, ask about it in your local grocery store. You can peel it by using the fruit peeling method I describe on page 13. After peeling, I generally cut the jicama into "sticks" and store it in water in the refrigerator. Depending on the time of year and starch content, the flavor can be much better after soaking or rinsing in cold water.

- **Kohlrabi** (see photo)—Kohlrabi is another vegetable that is well known in Europe and frequently grown in private gardens in the United States, but otherwise relatively unknown. To use, cut off the knobby exterior skin and slice or dice. It has a mild radish flavor and good crunch when it is fresh. It can be eaten steamed, but I prefer its flavor and texture raw.
- **Leek**—Leeks look like large green onions and have a similar flavor to green onion—maybe just a little milder. When I use leek I like to slice it in half end to end so that I can run water through the interior since they tend to have a little sandy grit inside. I love leek cooked in soup or in a cooked vegetable medley. It also tastes great finely sliced in salads where it adds a very mild onion-like flavor that most people find very inoffensive.
- **Mâche** (see photo)—In Germany they call this lovely crisp lettuce "Rapunzel." They say, it was the lettuce that got everyone in to so much trouble in the original Rapunzel fairy tale. Mâche is hard to find in the United States (at least where I live) but makes a wonderful salad, by itself or with other greens. It also tastes great in my colorful vegetable salad in the place of the Chinese cabbage.
- **Micro greens and sprouts**—While sprouts have been around for awhile, microgreens are a relatively new form of available greens. Microgreens look beautiful on top of any salad and can be a way to get a little green into other dishes. I think sprouts taste best on a sandwich. I love to use an alfalfa-radish blend on my Salad as a Sandwich, especially in combination with avocado. Sprouts can add variety to any salad, but don't tend to do well in salads where the dressing is tossed in with the salad.

- **Nasturtium leaves and flowers** (see photo)—A family I visited in Austria once served a salad that was just a platter of nasturtium leaves and flowers, attractively arranged. Nasturtium leaves and flowers are edible and have a lovely lightly spicy flavor like watercress. The great thing about Nasturtium is you can have it growing in your flower beds and no one will know that it is actually part of your vegetable garden.
- **Nopales** (see photo)—Native to Mexico, these dethorned pads of the prickly pear cactus have a slightly sour flavor and a texture similar to cucumber. Try a few diced in a salad like my Black Bean and Corn Salad (page 62).
- **Oak leaf lettuce**—This is a lesser known leaf lettuce with a lovely shape and nutty flavor. If you can find it, add it to any tossed salad.

- **Persimmon** (see photo)—Persimmons are sweet and mild and have good crunch. They should be eaten when they are crunchy, like an apple. If they are soft, they are overripe. To serve, peel them and slice, any direction. They are super easy to prepare since they have no seeds. Sliced through the equator they are gorgeous for any fruit tray, especially in the fall because of their pumpkin-orange color and pumpkin-like shape. Trader Joe's sells a delicious prepackaged persimmon salad that contains butter lettuce, a little kale, goat cheese crumbles, pomegranate seeds, roasted almonds, and roasted pumpkin seeds with a light pomegranate vinaigrette. Try making your own salad with persimmon sometime!
- **Pomegranate**—Pomegranate seeds, technically called "arils" can enliven almost any salad. The only problem is that the ones you can get at the store already removed from the fruit tend to be going bad, and it can be quite a bit of work to get them out. For an easy method, look up "remove pomegranate seeds wooden spoon" online.
- **Ramps, a.k.a Wild Leek**—This plant has a flavor that is a cross between onion and garlic and can be used in many different dishes where you would use green onion, leek, or chives. It is related to a plant called "bear leek" which is commonly eaten in the springtime in Europe (see page 86).
- **Rutabega**—This root vegetable looks a lot like turnip but has much milder flavor and light yellow flesh. Use if grated fresh on a salad, shaved, or roasted.
- **Sea beans**—sea beans is one name used for pieces of a succulent plant with a salty flavor. Use sparingly in salads instead of salt.
- **Turnbull pear**—A cross between an apple and a pear, it has a pear-like flavor but an apple-like crunch. These qualities make it perfect to use in salad.
- **Turnip**—Turnip looks like a large radish and has a similar sharp flavor. I like to buy lebanese-style pickled turnips to eat with falafel or use finely grated turnip in a salad instead of radish.
- **Watercress** (see photo)—Watercress was rated at the top of the list in a 2014 study of most nutrient-rich foods (just ahead of Chinese cabbage, Swiss chard, and spinach). It has a crisp texture and a radish-like flavor. Since the study came out I have seen watercress more frequently in grocery stores, usually in little clumps with roots and dirt. I bought one of these clumps, put it in a bowl, and was able to keep it alive several weeks by watering it a little every day or two. Watercress leaves are tasty on my Salad as a Sandwich and can be used on almost any salad. Read more about this study at: http://www.cdc.gov/pcd/issues/2014/13_0390.htm.

FREQUENTLY ASKED QUESTIONS

AREN'T YOU WORRIED ABOUT GETTING FOOD POISONING FROM TAINTED GREENS?

The amount of food poisoning cases related to greens—although well publicized—don't even begin to compare to the numbers of cases relating to meat, dairy, and cooked starches. As a certified food manager for twenty years, I intensively studied the principles behind keeping food safe. Based on the best knowledge we have, raw vegetables, fruits, and greens are some of the safest foods one can eat (more info below).

WHAT ARE THINGS I CAN DO TO KEEP MY SALADS SAFE DURING PREP?

Most food poisoning comes from either temperature abuse (letting something that has been cooked sit out too long or not get hot enough) or cross-contamination (dripping raw meat juices onto something that is to go into a salad would be an example). There are some simple things you can do to avoid these problems as you prepare salads:

- Keep cooked ingredients like cooked pasta or beans chilled. Don't let them sit out for long periods of time. This of course does not apply to dry beans (that have not been cooked) or to uncooked beans that you might be soaking or sprouting.
- Wash melons, cucumbers, and other vegetables and fruits with swift-running warm water before you use them. Scrub where appropriate.
- When preparing a salad that you will serve to a group, wash the produce, get out all the tools and ingredients you need, and then wear disposable gloves as you cut and prepare things. You should change your gloves if you touch your face or hair, open the fridge, or open a drawer. Correct glove use can help prevent the spread of viruses.
- If you are using raw meat or eggs in your meal, take care of preparing the meat or eggs and throwing away the packaging and shells before you get out any of your salad ingredients; or you can prepare your salad ingredients and set them aside before you get out your meat or eggs. This will help prevent cross-contamination.
- Keep a cutting board to use only for vegetables and fruit. I have a green one I use for that. If you never have raw meat in your kitchen, you probably don't need to do this, but if you do use raw meat sometimes, it's best long term if you know which cutting board is for the meat and which for the veggies. It's another strategy for preventing cross-contamination.

One of the really great things about eating green is that most of the time, your prep will all be "clean" stuff like raw veggies or fruit. When that's the case, you can rinse your cutting boards and knives with hot water and pat them dry with a paper towel, or just go straight onto cutting the next vegetable or fruit. This can save you time!

YOUR SEARED AHI SALAD CONTAINS UNDERCOOKED SEAFOOD. AREN'T YOU WORRIED ABOUT THIS?

When steak (whether fish or beef) is seared, the process of searing the outside kills the microorganisms that might have been transferred to the steak when it was cut. The inside (which hasn't been touched) remains "clean." The only problem with raw fish is that some types of fish can harbor parasites. Yellowfin (ahi) tends to not have parasites—that's why it's been used in sushi for centuries and is eaten raw all the time on many pacific islands. Based on my reading, I think there is greater risk in eating fish that has been mishandled during shipping or storage. That is why I recommend buying only very fresh-looking fish, using it the day you buy it, and keeping it cold while you take it home.

WHY DON'T MORE OF YOUR SALAD RECIPES CONTAIN MEAT OR EGGS OR CHEESE?

A large body of evidence convincingly shows that most of our health problems could be avoided entirely if our diets were much, much higher in vegetable protein and much lower in protein from animal sources including meat, eggs, and milk products. Some of the earliest research on this is described in the book *The China Study* by Dr. Colin Campbell. My dad and several of my uncles were research scientists, so I grew up surrounded by the scientific method. I am convinced that the research done by Dr. Campbell, his teams, and his associates over several decades was good science, done with the best research methods. In *The China Study,* Dr. Campbell relates that he grew up on a ranch and was sure that animal protein was the best protein. It took a lot of research to convince him that what his initial research was telling him could be right—that animal protein caused cancer in lab mice. He went on to participate in much more research on the subject and inspired others to do the same. If you want a quick overview on research being done currently I suggest this link: http://www.pcrm.org/health/ (Physician's Committee for Responsible Medicine—Health page). For an overview of Dr. Campbell's research and how it fits into other research, I suggest starting with this video: https://www.youtube.com/watch?v=LOEeTJY5zCM or reading the introduction to *The China Study*.

I like meat. I enjoy eggs. I love yogurt and gourmet cheeses. But I believe the research. I've decided to use meat, eggs, and cheese in my diet at times that they can make the most difference in terms of flavor. I don't put chicken or eggs on a salad any more merely for the sake of adding "protein" since I now know that the greens in the salad have plenty of protein (as long as I eat enough of them—see next FAQ). When I do eat meat, cheese, or eggs, I try to make sure they are high quality and will make a difference in my enjoyment of what I'm eating.

WHEN I'VE TRIED TO EAT JUST A SALAD FOR A MEAL, I DIDN'T GET FULL. HOW IS IT POSSIBLE TO EAT A SALAD FOR A MEAL AND NOT BE HUNGRY?

I used to think that all the time. I thought I couldn't really get full on a salad that wasn't loaded with lots of animal protein. The number one thing that changed my mind was finding out that lettuce actually has, per calorie, as much protein as steak. Since lettuce also has a lot of water and fiber, I knew that would mean I would have to eat more lettuce to get the same amount of protein as I would have eaten with a meal before, but I figured that was okay, since we all need more water and more fiber. I just needed to increase portion size and then make my salads interesting and delicious enough that I could get through a bigger portion. When I started drinking green smoothies regularly and craving greens it suddenly became much easier to eat a large salad because it tasted so good, even with less dressing and fewer toppings. Since then I've learned about how much lettuce I need in a salad to feel full and have found some bigger salad bowls that hold the amount I like to eat. Having the amount I like to eat already portioned out into a bowl makes it easier for me to keep eating until its gone. On some days when I'm really craving greens, I will make another half serving and eat that too. One thing to keep in mind—what counts as a "large" salad at a restaurant isn't necessarily going to fill you up. I recently ordered a "large" superfood salad at a popular chain. When I was done eating the "large" salad I felt like I had only had an appetizer. As it turns out, it only had about 2 ounces of greens—nowhere near enough to get me full. I typically eat salads with at least four to five ounces of greens (the same amount in one serving of my green smoothies) plus more veggies on top. Sometimes I eat up to ten ounces of a vegetable salad. Yesterday I started eating celery and didn't stop until I had eaten ten ounces of celery. That really surprised me because I really don't love celery!

If you are still feeling like a meal that is primarily salad just won't be satisfying, check out my suggestions at the end of this section.

DOESN'T IT TAKE A LOT OF PREP TIME TO CUT ALL THOSE VEGGIES AND PREP ALL THOSE GREENS?

I was talking to one of my nieces about the fact that it takes some time to get a big salad ready and she said "Yes, but by the time you are done with prep, you are done!" She's right—when I do a salad for dinner I make the salad, rinse my knife and cutting board, put anything I used to measure oil or dressing into the dishwasher, and sit down to eat with no need for cooking and hardly any cleanup when dinner is done.

The main thing that can make salad prep easier is having good tools. Really, all you need though is one good knife and a cutting board. Or a plate. It's amazing how much you can do with one good, serrated six-inch long knife. If you feel intimidated about getting started cutting vegetables, check out the videos on my website, www.MichelesGreenSmoothies.com. If you still feel making a salad will be a lot of work, check out my suggestions at the end of this section.

WHAT ABOUT THE EXPENSE OF BUYING ALL THAT FRESH PRODUCE?

One of my favorite quotes, attributed to Thomas Schlenstedt, says, "Whoever thinks being healthy is expensive, should try being sick sometime." It's easy to think that it won't be a problem to just eat whatever is cheap or whatever is easy, but the research being done says otherwise. If we keep eating the way we, as a culture, tend to eat, we will continue to have more of the "diseases of affluence"—diseases like type 2 diabetes and others. That being said, vegetables tend to be cheaper per pound than many milk and meat products. And they are definitely cheaper than most junk foods and processed foods. We just don't think about them that way. For more tips on feeling okay about buying produce, check out my list at the end of this section.

WHAT DO YOU THINK ABOUT ORGANICALLY GROWN PRODUCE?

I think the concept is a good one. Though, like anything else in the United States that has to do with nutrition, I think one has to be careful to separate the science from the advertising. Going back to the basics, plants get their nutrients from the soil. If the soil is depleted of nutrients, will the food we get from the plant be less nutritious? I think so. So, if one is trying to eat a high-nutrient diet, it probably makes sense to buy "organic" produce. Generally speaking, in the United States the emphasis in produce is on "does it look nice?" and not so much on "does it taste good?" I once had the chance to eat wild strawberries picked in a forest. As much as I like the strawberries I buy at the store, it seems to me that the amount of flavor packed into one tiny woodland strawberry is equal to or greater than the flavor in one giant grocery-store strawberry. Is flavor related to the nutritional benefit of a given type of produce? I personally believe it is. Since that is how I operate, I generally buy organic produce when my experience tells me the flavor will be better for that particular item.

WHY DON'T YOU TALK ABOUT SUPERFOODS?

I think the term "superfood" can be confusing. There are several definitions of the term. Some dismiss it as just a marketing term with no real meaning. Others define it as referring to foods that have a high nutrient to calorie ratio. My emphasis is on making eating choices that lead to eating more of the foods that have high nutrient value and cutting back on foods that we tend to refer to as "empty calories," but I don't know that the term "superfood" is necessarily always helpful in making those choices.

WHY DON'T MORE OF YOUR RECIPES CONTAIN KALE?

Kale is a green and, as such, is healthy. My problem with kale is I think it has gotten too much hype as a "superfood." In a 2014 scientific study ranking highly nutritious foods, kale came in six slots below romaine and ten slots below spinach. Like any research, the findings of this study might be reevaluated in the future; however, I think it is likely that kale has about the same nutritive value as eating most other leafy greens, including ones that aren't quite as tough and bitter. I personally think there is a "macho" aspect to kale—people think that because it is more bitter, it must be better for you. If you want to use kale, you can make it milder and more tender by freezing the leaves before use, heating them slightly in the microwave, or massaging them. For more on the research study mentioned above, read "Defining Powerhouse Fruits and Vegetables: A Nutrient Density Approach" by Jennifer Di Noia, PhD, found on the Center For Disease Control website at http://www.cdc.gov/pcd/issues/2014/13_0390.htm.

WHY DON'T YOU TALK ABOUT GROWING YOUR OWN GREENS? OR ABOUT SPROUTING?

If you have any kind of garden area, greens are—depending on your climate—one of the easiest and fastest things to grow. Sprouts are something you can do on your counter without any need for garden area and are packed with nutrients. So why don't I discuss that in this book? Two reasons. One is that I think the topics are easy to look up and learn about in other books and on the Internet. My main reason, though, is that I think if you are trying to change how you eat, how you prepare food, and how you think about food, you are already facing a huge challenge that takes extra time (at first) and extra mental and emotional energy—even with the tips and recipes I'm giving you to make it easier. If you aren't someone who is already growing a garden or sprouting, I think it's better to go ahead and try out my smoothies, salads, and other recipes using what you can get at the store until you get into a routine that works for you. At that point, if you have really started to Eat, Drink, and Be Green, you may want to find ways to decrease your costs and environmental impact by growing some of your own produce—but first things first.

WHAT ARE YOUR FAVORITE SALAD GREENS?

I really love butter lettuce and mâche. I also like romaine (when it isn't too bitter) and baby greens mixed with other lettuces. I think baby arugula can be deliciously nutty in the right setting, but it really has to be paired with the right ingredients.

DO YOU HAVE OTHER SUGGESTIONS FOR MAKING IT NOT SEEM SO OVERWHELMING TO MAKE A SALAD FOR DINNER?

When my husband and I started eating a salad most nights, there were times I just wanted to pull something out of the freezer and heat it up instead because it involved less thought than deciding on a salad. As we found salad recipes we liked, it became easier because we had certain "default" salads—salads we almost always had ingredients for that we knew would taste just fine on nights we were too tired to care. In this salad section, I have tried to provide recipes that could be good default salads as well as salads where some of the work could be done ahead. Below are some specific suggestions of how to use my salad recipes in ways that can make life simpler.

- Alternate more complicated salads with simpler ones.
- Before a busy day, make a salad that will keep (like my Classic Broccoli Salad) or one where the prep can be done ahead of time (like my European Layered Salad.) Romaine for Caesar salad can also be prepared twenty-four hours in advance and will be crisper if you do.
- Try some of the salad kits you can get at your grocery store. One of my favorite salad kits is the Taylor Farms

Asian Chopped Salad, often available at Costco. On a day I'm really hungry for greens, I can get through two-thirds of the 24-oz. package. (Just keep in mind that you may not need all of the dressing provided.)

- Always have some lettuce in your fridge. Lettuces like hearts of romaine and heads of butter lettuce will keep for 4–8 weeks.
- Prep fresh veggies when you have time and keep them in water in the fridge so they are nice and crisp and ready when you want to use them. I do this with jicama, carrots, and radishes.
- Have go-to salad recipes that you make often enough you don't have to think about them.
- Buy prewashed lettuce like the "Butter Bliss" that I recommend as a shortcut for my Butter Lettuce and Tomato Salad.
- If you are at the grocery store, buy a dense salad from the deli that you can take home and eat on top of greens for lunch or dinner. Southwestern, pasta, quinoa, kale, or Asian salads can work well for this.

I STILL HAVE A HARD TIME BELIEVING I COULD REALLY BE FULL AND SATISFIED EATING SALAD, BUT I KNOW I SHOULD TRY TO EAT HEALTHIER. DO YOU HAVE ANY OTHER THOUGHTS ABOUT THIS?

If you grew up in a meat-and-potatoes family or a pasta-and-bread family, it can be really difficult to make that paradigm shift. I grew up in a family that ate vegetables at every lunch and dinner, and it was still really hard for me. I think the primary thing is to recognize that it is a paradigm shift, that it's fine for it to seem hard! Chances are you have been used to eating the same types of foods for many, many years, so it makes sense for it to not be easy . . . but don't give up! If salad for dinner doesn't sound good to you now, maybe your body is letting you know that it needs a little more time to adjust. I think the most important thing is to drink your daily or three-times weekly green smoothie, and just see where it gets you. I do firmly believe that anyone who persists in drinking a full serving of intensely green smoothie at least three times a week will eventually start liking greens and vegetables better than they did. Below are some other things you can do to start getting more salads into your lunches and dinners:

- Salads usually sound better to people in the summer so try to start new habits with respect to Eating Green when the weather is warm.
- Start out by just having a side salad with every dinner or with nearly every dinner. Gradually increase the amount of salad you are having and decrease the amount of non-vegetable foods.
- Eat small items with your salad that have a "fun factor." Frozen appetizers like Spanakopita and pot stickers can work well for this. Or make my Stuffed Mushrooms (page 160).
- Make a fresh bread item to go with your salad (like my Blender Corn Muffins, page 151).
- Make individual salads for each person. Weigh the greens that go into the salad and make sure (for adults) there are at least four ounces of greens before adding toppings and other vegetables—this can help you make sure you are getting enough salad to fill up.
- Take enough time to eat that you "fill up the corners" and get pleasantly full.
- Once you know how much of a salad you have to eat to get full, buy some bigger individual salad bowls that you know hold the right amount of greens for you.
- Cut the greens smaller so that more will fit in your bowl. I do this by putting the greens in the bowl, then snipping them a few times with kitchen shears

(see video of this on my website, www.MichelesGreenSmoothies.com) and then adding more greens and snipping again.

- Alternate salads with some of my high-nutrient main dishes. When the weather gets colder, try doing more of my cooked vegetable recipes.
- Don't insist that other family member get full on greens if they aren't to that point. Just enjoy your greens and be patient. The feeling of being "full and happy" is an important part of any meal—whether it's greens or something else.

I HAVE A HARD TIME FEELING LIKE EATING MORE VEGGIES AND SALADS ISN'T GOING TO BREAK MY BUDGET. ANY OTHER SUGGESTIONS ON THAT?

- Buy your greens in whole heads and wash and prep them yourself. It's handy to buy the prewashed greens, but you can do your own prewashing. Greens that are washed and stored in plastic bags can keep several weeks.
- Cut out some of the processed and ready-to-eat snack foods you get (like chips) and replace them with inexpensive snacks like my Easy Chickpea Snack or hummus.
- Figure out the actual cost of greens-heavy meals you make compared to a meal made with meat and dairy or prepackaged foods.
- Check out ethnic grocery stores—some carry cheaper produce and most have fun vegetables to try.
- If you have neighbors with gardens, let them know that you are happy to use lettuce, zucchini, or other produce that might be getting away from them.
- If you don't have a vegetable garden, but do have a yard or balcony where you can grow things, plants like nasturtium (an edible flower—see page 78), basil, and zucchini can be tucked in almost anywhere.

SECTION 3

Main Dishes and Cooked Vegetables

- FROM ARTICHOKE TO ZUCCHINI SPAGHETTI
- RECIPES
- FREQUENTLY ASKED QUESTIONS

FROM ARTICHOKE TO ZUCCHINI SPAGHETTI

Most of my life, my parents have had a huge garden—a hundred tomato plants, rows of corn, and enough raspberries to share with the whole neighborhood. The most awaited moment in spring was always the first ripe raspberry; in summer, the first cob of corn and the first ripe tomato. In Germany, they have preserved this sense of anticipation as a culture. In early spring there is the *Bärlauchzeit* ("wild leek time") and then the *Spargelzeit* ("asparagus time") and then in the late fall *Das Grünkohlessen*, which, roughly translated, means "the eating of the green." The green they have in mind here is a type of kale which was traditionally picked after the first frost, making it less bitter. During the *Grünkohl* season every year, people go on trips to towns near where *Grünkohl* is grown and eat as much of the cooked green stuff and accompanying potatoes and sausage as they can. Across the border in the Netherlands, they also get excited about *Boerenkool* ("farmer cabbage") and use it in certain *stamppot* recipes.

When spring finally comes to Europe, it's all about *Bärlauch*—a type of wild leek. All through Germany during *Bärlauch* season, people gather the herb wild or in parks and use it in all kinds of salads and sauces. As *Bärlauch* season ends, the "asparagus time" begins and the whole country seems to go crazy. Every restaurant has a new menu of *Spargel* dishes and everyone eats their fill, because once the German-grown special white asparagus is gone for the summer, it's gone.

It's interesting to observe a culture where the yearly coming of a certain season still inspires a festival atmosphere and a joyful sense of anticipation ... and it's all for some vegetables! In this chapter I've tried to assemble a wide variety of cooked vegetable dishes that you can get excited about—from Artichoke to Zucchini Spaghetti! While we may not be used to thinking of a meal in terms of multiple vegetable dishes, two cooked vegetables and a side salad can make a great meal, summer or winter. One of my favorite summer menus is Parmesan Zucchini with Betty's Cucumbers, Garlic Grilled Green Beans and fresh sliced garden tomatoes. In the winter I might do Baked Sweet Potato with Walt's Coleslaw and Roasted Onions. Or maybe Christmas Sprouts with some German red cabbage (just heated from the jar) and a small Butter Lettuce and Tomato Salad . . . yum! It all sounds good—I think I am getting hungry!

Scattered in among all the great cooked vegetable recipes are some fun main dishes and easy, filling soups that taste good, summer or winter. I love how full and happy I feel after I make my Pad Thai or the satisfying feeling of eating Tom's Cabbage Borscht or Sharla's Easy Minestrone, maybe with a slice of my Super Easy No-Knead Bread. Okay, now I really am getting hungry! I'm off to make some Puréed Parsnips . . .

artichoke

I grew up eating artichokes and they are one of the foods my family loves. I loved eating them as a kid because they were finger food. It was fun to peel off each leaf and see how much of the soft inner part I could scrape off with my teeth. It takes a while to eat an artichoke and I think eating artichokes taught me how to slow down and enjoy a meal.

INGREDIENTS	PER PERSON
artichoke	1
bay leaf	1 large
salt	1 tsp.
butter	2 Tbsp.
mayonnaise	2 Tbsp.
Serves:	1

INSTRUCTIONS

1. Thoroughly rinse artichokes to remove any grit. Cut off the stem at the base. Using a large serrated knife (like a bread knife), cut off the top 1–1½ inches of the artichoke leaves. Set the artichoke on the cutting board with the newly created flat side down. Cut the artichoke in half by cutting down through the stem.

2. Remove the fuzzy part and the smallest leaves at the center of each artichoke half. This is easiest to do using a grapefruit spoon.

3. Immediately place the prepared artichoke halves in a large cooking pot. Add enough water to cover them, then go on to preparing any other artichokes. (Placing them immediately in water will help keep the artichoke halves from going brown).

4. Add the bay leaf and the salt. Make sure there is enough water to generously cover all the artichoke halves.

5. Bring the water to a boil. After it reaches a boil, reduce heat and cover.

6. Simmer 25–30 minutes. Artichoke is done when small outer leaves pull off very easily and the heart (where you removed the fuzz) is easily pierced with a fork.

7. Prepare dipping sauce: Heat butter until just barely melted. Allow it to cool slightly and then mix it with the mayo. Set an extra serving bowl on the table for discarding the artichoke leaves.

TIPS

- You can watch a video on artichoke prep and also learn another method for preparing them on my website, www.MichelesGreenSmoothies.com.
- I don't always love the flavor of bay leaf in things—I think it is easy to get too much. In this recipe, though, the bay leaf simply enhances the artichoke flavor. One leaf is enough for up to four artichokes.
- Try to make sure that all parts of the artichoke are under water as they cook. Any parts of the artichoke that are not submerged will remain tough.
- If you haven't eaten a whole artichoke before, you eat it by removing one leaf at a time, dipping the end in the sauce, and then using your lower front teeth to strip off the soft inner part of the leaf, leaving behind the fibrous part of the leaf. The outermost leaves are too tough and have to be discarded. The innermost leaves are only edible at the base. Once all the leaves are removed, what you have left is the "heart." Cut it into pieces and eat with dipping sauce.
- You can add a tiny bit of mustard or a squeeze of lemon juice for a variation on the dipping sauce.
- Artichokes contain compounds that make other foods eaten with them seem sweeter. Try serving artichokes with boiled potatoes and Butter Lettuce and Tomato Salad. The potatoes and salad will both taste uniquely good after a bite of artichoke. Artichokes can be eaten hot or cold.

baked potato with vegetarian chili

Baked potatoes sometimes get dismissed because they are a "carb." The fact remains, though, that they are also a vegetable and are high in vitamins and minerals, although not as high as most greens. I like to bake several extra potatoes when I make them for dinner and freeze them to use alongside a salad for lunch on a winter day (instructions below).

INSTRUCTIONS

1. Choose medium size Russet baking potatoes. Wash and scrub them, and then pierce each potato several times with a sharp paring knife.

2. Preheat oven to 425 degrees. To speed up cooking time, microwave the potatoes until they are hot—1½–2 minutes per potato that you are heating. Transfer the hot potatoes to the preheated oven and bake for 15 minutes.

3. Turn the oven down to 325 degrees and bake for an additional 20 minutes (40 minutes if you didn't microwave them).

4. Check for doneness by squeezing the potatoes with a hot pad. They should feel very soft.

5. Remove the potatoes from the oven and massage each potato with a hot pad to soften the interior. Do this right away, and then make a cut along the length of each potato and squeeze each one open. This releases the steam and will help the potatoes have the fine, dry texture that makes a good baked potato.

6. Serve topped with vegetarian chili (recipe on page 91), snipped green onions, or other toppings of your choice.

TIPS

- I often wondered if piercing the potato is really necessary. It turns out it is necessary, but mostly in the late fall and early winter when the potatoes have been freshly harvested and have a very high water content. Later in the year potatoes have a lower water content and are less likely to explode if you don't pierce them.
- Baking potatoes at a high temperature at first helps develop the chewy skin and creamy interior that make a baked potato a baked potato. It's important to do the high temperature at the start and the lower temperature second until they are done rather than reversing the sequence. Using a high temperature at the end tends to make them explode.
- Larger potatoes will take more time to cook—more time to get hot in the microwave, more time in the oven. I like to use smaller potatoes because they cook faster.
- Leftover baked potatoes that are refrigerated just don't taste the same the next day, but I recently discovered that freezing them works great. When thawed, they tasted very nearly the same as they did freshly baked. To freeze: cut open the potatoes as described in step 5 and squeeze them open. Allow them to cool to room temperature. Put each potato in a size-appropriate container, top with chili, put on the lid and put in the freezer. You can also put several potatoes without toppings in a pan to freeze and then bag them once they are frozen. When ready to eat, transfer a potato from the container or bag to a microwaveable bowl or plate. Microwave on 50 percent power until heated through.

VEGETARIAN CHILI

INGREDIENTS	1X	2X
yellow onion	½ onion	1 onion
V-8 juice	1 (5.5-oz.) can	1 (11.5-oz.) can
maple syrup	1½ tsp.	1 Tbsp.
chili powder	1–2 tsp.	2–4 tsp.
dry granulated garlic	1 tsp.	2 tsp.
cumin	1 tsp.	2 tsp.
ground oregano	¼ tsp.	½ tsp.
canned or cooked pinto beans, drained and rinsed	1 (15-oz.) can	2 (15-oz.) cans or 1 (30-oz.) can
fresh tomatoes	6 oz.	12 oz.
Serves:	2	4 to 5

INSTRUCTIONS

1. Chop the onion and sauté in a small amount of oil with a sprinkle of salt. Sauté until onion looks translucent. Add all the other ingredients except the fresh tomatoes. Simmer sauce and beans until the vegetable juice has mostly evaporated and the sauce has become very thick. Reduce heat to low until ready to eat.

2. Meanwhile, weigh, wash, and quarter the tomatoes. Process them in a blender or food processor until they are chopped but not completely puréed.

JUST BEFORE EATING, stir the tomatoes into the chili. Serve over baked potatoes.

TIPS AND VARIATIONS

- The onion amount is not exact in this recipe because it doesn't matter too much if you have a little more or a little less.
- The tomatoes can be simmered with the chili but adding them fresh at the last minute preserves nutrients. You can of course reheat the chili or simmer the tomatoes with the beans if desired.

baked sweet potato

I had never had baked sweet potato until I had it at a restaurant near Cedar Breaks, Utah. Until then I had always had it boiled. I was surprised how different the texture was when it was baked. At that restaurant it was served sprinkled with cinnamon and with melted butter on it—you could add your own salt and pepper. Since then my favorite way to eat sweet potato has been baked, split open and topped with cinnamon, fresh ground black pepper, and a little salt and butter. Someone I knew made her French toast using salt, pepper, and cinnamon. She said the salt and pepper were there for the eggs and the cinnamon for the toast. I think the same principle works here—the cinnamon is for the "sweet" part of the sweet potato and the salt, pepper, and butter for the "potato" part. If you have never had a baked sweet potato, give it a try. Paired with a small salad it makes a very satisfying and nutritious winter meal.

INSTRUCTIONS

1. Choose medium size or small sweet potatoes (the kind with dark orange flesh, sometimes called yams). Wash them and prick the flesh with a knife.

2. Bake in microwave or oven.

MICROWAVE: four to five minute for one potato, an additional 2–3 minutes for each additional potato. Check for doneness by squeezing the potatoes (protect your hand with a hot pad).

OVEN: set potatoes straight on the oven rack and bake at 400 degrees for 30–45 minutes or until potatoes are easy to "squish." You may want to put a piece of foil on the rack below the potatoes since some sweet juices can drip from the potato during baking and burn onto your oven.

3. Cut the potato in half lengthwise. Sprinkle with cinnamon. Serve with butter, salt, and fresh ground pepper.

TIPS

- Look up "sweet potato nutrition" online for interesting information on why sweet potatoes are good for you.
- When I bake regular russet potatoes, I like to start them in the microwave (so they cook faster) and finish them in the oven so they get the nice crispy skin and fluffy interior. Sweet potatoes seem to turn out just fine "baking" them the whole time in the microwave. For me, this makes baked sweet potato a "convenience food"—they can be stored on the counter for weeks and cook in just a few minutes.
- There is no need to oil your sweet potatoes or wrap them in foil.

busy-night stir-fry

On busy nights, or nights when I don't know quite what to make and am not in the mood for a salad, I make a stir-fry. I often do a stir-fry right before I need to go to the grocery store because it is a good way (and a tasty way!) to use up odds and ends of vegetables I have in my fridge.

INGREDIENTS	1X
sesame oil	1 Tbsp.
minced garlic (fridge)	1 tsp.
crushed ginger (fridge)	1 tsp.
frozen stir-fry mix	10–16 oz mix
broccoli stems or matchstick carrots (optional)	~4 oz
sliced mushrooms (optional)	7–8 oz
bean sprouts, chard, chinese cabbage or baby bok choi	5–10 oz.
stir-fry sauce (optional—see Tip)	2–3 Tbsp.
toasted sesame oil or mongolian fire oil (optional)	a few drops
pre-cooked brown rice (optional)	½ cup per person
Serves:	3 to 5

INSTRUCTIONS

1. Preheat the sesame oil in a large skillet or wok. Add the garlic and ginger and stir with the oil until they start to cook. Add the frozen stir-fry. (If the stir-fry includes a packet of meat or shrimp, cook that before adding the vegetables.) Stir-fry the vegetables over highest heat until they are thawed. If using matchstick carrots, broccoli stems, or other hard vegetables, add them next.

2. Add the sliced mushrooms (if using) and then the bean sprouts, chard, chinese cabbage or bok choi. You can add quite a lot of any of these and they will cook down. After you add them, it can be helpful to put a lid on your sauté pan or wok (even a lid that doesn't fit) for a couple of minutes to trap some of the steam and help the leafy vegetables to cook down a little, making them easier to stir in.

3. Add the packet from your frozen stir-fry if you have one or add some stir-fry sauce. Add a little, then taste the stir-fry to see if it needs more. Proceed cautiously (don't add too much at once), but also work quickly so that the vegetables don't get overdone. Add a little toasted sesame oil, if desired, for more flavor or mongolian fire oil for more "zip."

SERVE immediately over brown rice, or just eat it straight.

TIPS AND VARIATIONS

- Some of the vegetables I use up in a stir-fry include stems of chard or baby bok choi that I used in smoothies, broccoli stem pieces that I didn't want to use in a salad, matchstick carrots that are starting to get dry, zucchini that didn't get used up for another recipe, a small piece of onion that I want to get out of the fridge, green onions that won't keep much longer, and so on. Sometimes I have enough that I don't need to use my frozen stir-fry mix, but I find that using the frozen mix makes it easier to get started and means I will have enough to make a meal.
- You can use lots of different frozen mixes. I use those that are just vegetables or vegetables with a small amount of meat. One that I like is the Trader Joe Shrimp Stir-fry (16-oz.) It has a nice combination of vegetables and a very mild seasoning. You can use the shrimp or leave it out depending on preference.
- Some frozen mixes include a sauce packet or seasoning packet and some just have vegetables. Regardless of what packet comes with the mix, I always start with the sesame oil, garlic, and ginger—it adds freshness and a boost of flavor without being overwhelming. Then I decide if I want to use the included sauce or use my own. I always keep stir-fry sauce, toasted sesame oil, and mongolian fire oil in my fridge. You can instead use soy sauce plus a little agave or pineapple juice for sweetness.
- Brown rice takes so long to cook that I like to either buy the frozen brown rice or make a big batch and freeze it to use for meals like this one or for Carolee's Baked Chimichangas (page 95).
- I don't include larger batch sizes for this recipe because doing a bigger batch would require a really big wok or two frying pans. When stir-frying, it is critical to have enough surface area that the water can evaporate as you cook the vegetables. If you put too many stir-fry vegetables in one pan, the juices from the vegetables can collect and turn the recipe into soup. It's also important to keep the heat turned up so the juices can evaporate.
- For more ideas of what to put in a stir-fry, visit a Mongolian BBQ—the kind where you go through a food bar and choose your own ingredients.
- Stir-fry (if not overcooked) reheats well, and I like using it for a next-day lunch.

carolee's baked chimichangas

My sister loved growing and eating lots of vegetables long before I did. She frequently made this yummy baked chimichanga recipe for her family and guests, and often used her own garden cabbage and onions in the recipe. I love eating these but especially love the fact that I can freeze them and have easy, individual meals to pull out and heat up!

INGREDIENTS	1X	2X
petite diced tomatoes	1 (15-oz.) can	2 (15-oz.) cans
black or pinto beans	1 (15-oz.) can	2 (15-oz.) cans
sweet white or red onion	¼–½ onion	½–1 whole onion
sliced black olives (optional)	1 (4-oz.) can	2 (4-oz.) cans
diced green chiles	1 (4-oz.) can	2 (4-oz.) cans
pre-cooked brown rice	¾ cup	1½ cups
ground oregano	¼ tsp.	½ tsp.
ground cumin	¼ tsp.	½ tsp.
dry granulated garlic	1 tsp.	2 tsp.
shredded cabbage	7 oz. (about 3 cups)	14 oz. coleslaw mix
white Mexican or shredded cheddar cheese (optional)	1 cup	2 cups
9 or 10-inch whole-grain tortillas	1 pkg. (10-12/pkg.)	2 pkgs. (10-12/pkg.)
Filling:	6 cups (volume)	12 cups (volume)
Makes:	about 10	about 20

INSTRUCTIONS

1. Open the tomatoes and pour them into a strainer. Allow them to drain while you do the other prep. Reserve the juice from the tomatoes for another use if desired. Drain and rinse the beans. Chop the onion and drain the olives. Add the onion, olives, and all the other ingredients (except the tortillas) to the mixing bowl and stir to combine.

2. Cook or warm the tortillas (see Tips). While they are still warm, add the filling: scoop ½–¾ cup filling onto the middle of a tortilla. Fold one side over the filling, then fold in the top and the bottom ends. Finish by folding the other side to tightly enclose the filling.

3. Place on a lined baking tray with the seam side down. Bake at 425 for 15 minutes. Top with Guacamole (page 168) or serve with Brazilian Heart of Palm Salad (page 49).

TIPS

- For the cabbage (1x recipe), you can use half of a 14-oz. bag of coleslaw mix.
- I like to use the whole wheat ready-to-cook tortillas for this. You can also use pre-cooked tortillas or any kind of wrap.
- These freeze and reheat really well. I usually wrap each leftover chimi in plastic wrap and put them all in a freezer-grade storage bag. To reheat in the microwave: Remove the packaging, and wrap each chimi in a paper towel. Microwave on 50 percent power until heated through.

cauliflower with buttered crumbs

It was when I was living in Germany that I first learned that soft-cooked vegetables can also taste good in the right context. In this typical European recipe, the whole head of cauliflower takes on a casserole-like texture and the buttered crumbs give it a rich flavor.

INGREDIENTS	1X	4X
cauliflower	1 head, about 24 oz.	4 heads, about 6 lbs.
Ritz-style crackers	20 crackers or 2 oz. (~⅓ cup crumbs)	8 oz. (~1⅓ cups crumbs)
butter	1 cube (½ cup, 4 oz.)	1 lb.
Serves as main dish:	2–3	8–12

INSTRUCTIONS

1. Rinse your cauliflower, leaving the head whole and trimming the base as needed. Add about a half inch of water to a cooking pot with a diameter just slightly bigger than the cauliflower. Lightly salt the water and add the whole cauliflower. (For large batch, cut cauliflower into florets.)

2. Bring the water to a boil. Reduce heat and cover the pot. Steam until the cauliflower can be easily cut with a serving spoon (this is slightly more done than fork-tender.) This should take 20–25 minutes.

3. While the cauliflower cooks, crumble the crackers. I like to do this by putting them in a sealed heavy-duty plastic bag and squishing them with my hand or with the bottom of a measuring cup. Melt the butter in a sauté pan and stir the crumbs into the melted butter. Keep on low heat until the cauliflower is done.

4. Transfer the cauliflower to a serving dish and spoon the buttered crumbs over the top. Keep the cooking water if desired for the optional sauce (recipe below). Serve the cauliflower immediately or keep warm in a 300 degree oven until ready to serve—this will keep the crumbs from getting soggy.

5. Serve like a casserole by scooping pieces out of the cauliflower with a serving spoon. Serve with Colorful German Salad or another salad.

WUPPERTAL
NÜRNBERG
BERLIN

OPTIONAL SAUCE

It is very common in Germany to make a light white sauce to serve over vegetables. You can make this sauce and serve it in addition to or instead of the crumbs:

1. Melt 2 tablespoons butter in the sauté pan. Stir in 3–4 tablespoons whole wheat flour to form a paste. Cook on low until this butter/flour "roux" starts to smell a bit like baked sugar cookies and have a crumbly texture.

2. Measure the water left from cooking the cauliflower. If there is more that 2 2¼ cups, turn the pot on to boil until enough water evaporates to leave just the required amount.

3. Add about ½ cup of the cooking water to the roux and stir until smooth and thickened. Gradually stir in the remaining water and cook over medium heat until the sauce thickens, stirring frequently. Taste the sauce and add salt as needed and a little freshly ground pepper. To make the sauce even better, Germans will add a little cream and dash of freshly grated nutmeg. Transfer the sauce to a serving bowl or pitcher and present alongside the cauliflower.

TIPS AND VARIATIONS

- It's important to put the crumbs on the cauliflower just before serving so that they don't get soggy. This can be a great dish to take to a pot luck, but if you do, take the buttered crumbs separately, reheat them in the microwave (if needed), and spoon them over the cauliflower just before serving. If you only need one serving or don't plan to eat the whole cauliflower in one sitting, scale back the buttered crumbs. When you reheat the cauliflower, do new crumbs to go with it.
- Carrot variation: Cook 1½ pounds of baby carrots or carrot sticks until tender. Prepare the crumbs and set them aside. Make the white sauce as directed above (using cooking liquid from the carrots), and pour it over the carrots in a baking dish, then distribute the crumbs over the top. Bake at 375 degrees for 20 minutes. If desired, you can add 1 teaspoon dry granulated onion and 1 teaspoon prepared horseradish to the sauce before you pour it over the carrots.

christmas sprouts

In England, "sprouts" (what we call brussels sprouts) are a traditional part of Christmas dinner. That being said, people in England seem to have a love-hate relationship with brussels sprouts—probably in the same way that people in the United States have a love-hate relationship with Thanksgiving sweet potatoes. Most Americans also don't love brussels sprouts, and I think this comes in part from how they are cooked. Many of our parents or grandparents grew up eating mushy vegetables—either because they came from a can or because that was just "the right way" to cook them. In the seventies, it became popular to serve vegetables barely cooked and still crunchy. This was a good trend because shorter cooking times preserve more nutrients . . . On the other hand, depending on how they are prepared, crunchy "cooked" vegetables can be just as unappealing as mushy ones. While not my favorite vegetable, I think brussels sprouts can be quite good when cooked until tender—not crispy, not mushy. If you have never had them like that, give this recipe a try. Maybe it will become one of your winter traditions!

INGREDIENTS	1X	2X
brussels sprouts	12 oz.	24 oz.
butter or butter/olive oil blend	¾–1 ounce or 1½–2 Tbsp.	1½–2 oz. or 3–4 Tbsp.
chopped pecans or hazelnuts	¼ oz.	½ oz.
sauté pan size	10 inches or larger	12 inches or larger
As side dish serves:	2	4 to 5

INSTRUCTIONS

1. Prepare the sprouts by trimming the ends, removing any bruised or loose outer leaves and cutting them in half.

2. Place them in a covered sauté pan along with about half an inch of water. Bring the water to a boil. Reduce heat and simmer until sprouts are tender when pierced by a fork. If it looks like you will run out of water in the pan before the sprouts get done, add more.

3. Drain any water remaining in the pan. Add the chopped nuts and the butter or butter/oil blend and return the pan to the heat until the butter melts. Move the sprouts around in the butter until they are coated, and then arrange them in a single layer, cut-side down.

4. Continue cooking with lid off over medium heat until sprouts are lightly brown on the cut side. Sprinkle lightly with dry granulated onion and salt if desired. Transfer to serving dish.

TIPS

- If Brussels sprouts burn, they smell terrible. If you get a loose leaf or two in your pan while cooking them, those leaves can get overdone and also smell terrible, even though all the other sprouts are fine. You and your family will probably feel more like eating them if you smell browned butter than if you smell overdone greens. . . . Just something to keep in mind when preparing this recipe.

dave's winter squash

My brother has become famous for bringing his tasty baked squash casserole to family parties all winter and it generally takes the place of sweet potatoes on our Thanksgiving table. In this recipe, the dill and squash flavors seem to mutually mellow each other so that some people who think they don't like winter squash, or dill, end up liking the combination.

INGREDIENTS	1X	5X
winter squash (see Tips)	whole squash weighing 1½–2 lbs.	whole squash weighing 7½–10 lbs.
dry granulated onion	1–2 Tbsp.	¼–½ cup
dry dill weed	½–1 tsp.	2½–5 tsp.
chopped pecans or whole grain crackers	½–1 oz.	2½–5 oz.
Makes:	about 2 cups	about 10 cups
Serves:	2 to 4	10 to 20

INSTRUCTIONS

1. Cut each squash in half and scoop out the seeds. (An easy way to cut a squash is explained in Tips.) Place the squash halves on a foil-lined baking sheet, cut side down. Bake at 300 degrees for 1½–2 hours (depending on how large the squash is). The squash will be very soft when done.

2. Allow the squash to cool slightly and then scoop the flesh of the squash into a mixing bowl (discard the shell). You can mix the squash by hand using a potato masher or you can use the blade attachment on a stand mixer. Add the dry onion and dry dill, and mix until all the lumps are gone.

3. Spread the squash into a casserole dish, about two inches thick. Spread the nuts or crumbs over the top and bake at 350 degrees until hot (20–40 minutes).

TIPS

- Purchasing winter squash: You can use sweetmeat, butternut, hubbard, turban, hokkaido or any squash that has dark orange, relatively dry flesh (the dryer the better). 1½–2 pounds whole raw squash yields about 1 pound cooked squash.
- Cutting squash: Stand the squash on a cutting board with the stem end up. Insert a sharp paring knife just below the stem with the knife point directed toward

the center of the squash. Cut down through the squash, rotating the squash as needed so that you are always cutting down toward the cutting board. Continue cutting until you get all the way around, and then split the squash apart.

- While there are lots of different ways to cook squash, cooking it low and slow as recommended in this recipe results in dryer, tastier squash. If the flesh of your squash still seems very wet when you scoop it out, you can transfer it from the mixing bowl to a colander lined with a paper towel. Let it stand this way (over a bowl to collect the liquid) for an hour while it cools or overnight in the fridge and then transfer it back to a mixing bowl and add in the seasonings. This will lead to a dryer finished product.
- You can refrigerate or freeze the squash dish before heating it in step three. Keeping the casserole in the fridge for a day before baking and serving allows more time for the flavors to blend.

european lentil soup

I first had this lentil soup in Switzerland. Unlike most lentil soups I have had in the United States, this soup is light and emphasizes the vegetables. In this soup the lentils play a role similar to rice in a chicken and rice soup. You can make this recipe for one person, so it's great for an easy meal on a day that you just need some soup.

INGREDIENTS	1X	4X
dry lentils, any color	2 oz. or ¼ cup	8 oz. or 1 cup
water for soaking	1 cup	1 quart
celery root, finely diced	2 oz. or ~½ cup	8 oz. or 2 cups
matchstick carrots	2 oz. or ~¾ cup	8 oz. or 3 cups
vegetable broth	1½ cups	1½ quarts
fresh chives or parsley	6–8 stems chives or 2–3 stems parsley	1 package chives or half bunch parsley
Makes:	1½ cups	6 cups
Serves:	1	4

INSTRUCTIONS

1. Rinse the lentils, and then put them in water to soak for at least 4 hours or up to 24 hours. Pour the lentils into a strainer to drain.

2. Finely dice your celery root. Heat a little butter or olive oil in a saucepan with a lid that will fit the batch of soup you are making (1x recipe can be made in a sauté pan; 4x recipe will need at least a two-quart sauce pan). Sauté the celery in the oil or butter over medium-high heat. Cook until celery root is lightly browned—about 5 minutes.

3. Add the carrots and soaked lentils, and sauté an additional 5 minutes on medium.

4. Add the broth and bring to a boil. Reduce heat and simmer soup covered for 10–15 minutes or until carrots are tender.

5. Pour into serving dishes and add finely snipped chives or parsley to each bowl.

TIPS

- Soaked lentils don't tend to go mushy when cooked in a soup like cooked lentils often do, but do require some planning ahead. As a time saver for future batches, you can soak extra lentils and freeze them in premeasured amounts. Two ounces (about ¼ cup) dry lentils yield around five ounces (about ¾ cup) soaked lentils. I don't recommend using the precooked lentils you can buy now. They often have other flavorings added, have too much salt, and are a little mushy.

- Matchstick carrots (see page 36) make this recipe very easy, but you can julienne or finely slice your own.
- My current favorite brand of vegetable stock for this recipe is Full Circle brand. It is sold in one-liter boxes. You can use refrigerated vegetable stock concentrate instead (the kind that comes in a small bottle as a paste), but it is easy to get too much. If using broth concentrate, start by using half as much as would need to make the amount of broth called for in the recipe and add more if you need it.
- A similar lentil soup is traditional in Turkey and is called *Mercimek Corbasi*. To make this variation, use onion instead of celery root and purée the soup after it is cooked. Instead of the chives or parsley, season lightly with cumin and black pepper. Serve with lemon wedges to squeeze into the soup. It is traditional to use red lentils for this soup.

falafel with salads

Ever since my first trip to the Middle East in 1994 I have tried to come up with the perfect falafel recipe. I have tried various recipes and made up my own but they never lived up to what I had eaten there . . . until now. These are crunchy on the outside, creamy in the middle, and not too dense. Even better, they taste just as good pan fried as deep fried.

INGREDIENTS	1X	2X
dry garbanzo beans (dry weight)	4 oz.	8 oz. (half of a 1-lb. bag)
hot water for soaking	1½ cups	3 cups
dry granulated onion	1 Tbsp.	2 Tbsp.
salt	¼ tsp.	½ tsp.
ground cumin	1½ tsp.	3 tsp.
ground coriander	2 tsp.	4 tsp.
ground black pepper	⅛ tsp.	¼ tsp.
toasted sesame oil	1 tsp.	2 tsp.
minced garlic (fridge)	1 tsp.	2 tsp.
Total "dough":	9 oz.	18 oz.
Total falafel:	about 18	about 34
Servings:	about 6	about 12

INSTRUCTIONS

1. Rinse the dry garbanzo beans and place them in a container with the water to soak overnight or for at least 10 hours.

2. Pour the garbanzo beans into a colander and allow them to drain for at least 15 minutes so that all the water drips off. Meanwhile measure out all the dry ingredients.

3. Place approximately half of the garbanzo beans in the food processor. Process until they are very finely ground and smooth—like hummus, but dryer.

4. Add the remaining garbanzo beans, the dry seasonings, and the sesame oil and garlic. Process just until the garbanzo beans added second are about the size of sesame seeds or resemble bread crumbs. There should be no pieces larger than a lentil.

5. Scoop falafel using a half-ounce scoop (see page 5) and cook using one of the methods under cooking methods below. Regardless of cooking method, it's important to not compress the falafel too much as you shape them; otherwise, they will be too dense. Set cooked falafel on paper towels to absorb any extra oil.

6. Serve hot with salads (see serving suggestions below) or freeze to use another day.

COOKING METHODS:

- Electric griddle: Heat your griddle to 400 degrees. Drizzle olive oil generously over the surface. Use the cookie scoop to drop balls of dough onto the griddle, and then use the back of a pancake turner to gently flatten them so that they are slightly under half an inch thick. Cook until they are a nice, dark even brown color on the underneath side and then turn and repeat. Please note that they will only go brown and crispy if they are touching the hot olive oil. You may need to add more olive oil when you turn them. I like this method because it's easy to see what temperature the griddle is set to, and as long as there is enough olive oil, they come out with great crunch! They are also a handy shape to put in a pita pocket. I think this is the easiest method, and it also involves the least amount of oil.
- Frying Pan: Pour oil into the pan ¼–½ inch deep. Heat the oil over medium-high until it starts to "shimmer." You can test the oil by dropping in a crumb of the dough. If the oil is ready, the dough should float to the top almost immediately and bubbles should form around it. Scoop a ball of dough and flatten it slightly. Set it into the hot oil. You can do several balls at once, but if you do too many the oil temperature will drop and they won't cook well. Turn the balls over once the first side is a deep, even brown.
- Deep Fryer: Use a scoop to portion the dough but use your fingers to gently shape it into a ball (without compacting it too much). Gently lower balls into the oil when it is ready (see Frying Pan method above for a way to test the oil.) Should take about 2–3 minutes total.

SERVING SUGGESTIONS:

Falafel generally are served on a plate with salads or in a pita pocket. When eaten on a pita, it is customary to open the pita pocket, fill it with salads and vegetables, and then top it with fresh, warm falafel and your sauce of choice. More recently people have been making falafel wraps where you lay the falafel down the center of the wrap on top of hummus, then add toppings. Whether you eat it on a plate, in a wrap, or on a pita, here are some salads and toppings that can go well with your warm falafel. (You can find more ideas by doing an image search on "falafel" or "falafel bar.")

- Even though we think of coleslaw as American, the Walt's Coleslaw recipe in this book goes perfectly with falafel and is not too different from cabbage salads served at falafel bars.
- Carrot salads can often be found in falafel bars in the Middle East. To make a simple carrot salad, use matchstick carrots or grated carrot. Drizzle with olive oil and add half as much lemon juice as olive oil. Sprinkle generously with sweet paprika and stir. For a spicy salad, add a dash of cayenne. Alternatively you can use the vinaigrette recipe on page 55. Carrot salads taste best if they have time to marinate—up to 24 hours in the refrigerator.
- Tabbouleh is a wonderful Middle Eastern salad that goes nicely on a falafel plate. My sister-in-law Kathleen started making tabbouleh almost thirty years ago before most other people in my area had even heard of it. Now you can often buy it premade at a grocery store deli. You can also find lots of recipes for it online.
- Some falafel recipes call for finely chopped parsley or cilantro in the falafel. I prefer to put mine on my falafel wrap or pita as a garnish. You can put out whole springs or finely chop to sprinkle on your falafel salad plate.
- Fresh sliced cucumbers and tomatoes go well with falafel. You can instead use Betty's Marinated Cucumbers, page 46, or Colorful Vegetable Salad, page 50. If

you happen to have pico de gallo on hand, that can go well too. Pico de gallo, while coming from Tex-Mex tradition, is not very different from Mediterranean style salads.

- Falafel are often served with pickled vegetables of various kinds. I really like the hot-pink lebanese-style turnips (available in specialty markets and some grocery stores) that are a traditional part of a falafel bar. These pickled turnips look strange and smell strong but have a pleasant mild flavor.
- Some kind of sauce is nice to have (though not absolutely essential if you use coleslaw on your falafel plate or in your wrap). A tahini sauce is traditional but I prefer hummus (see recipe page 170) or a simple tzatziki like the one in the Tips on page 48.

TIPS

- It works best to use garbanzo beans that were purchased recently. Beans that are several years old can work, but can take much longer to soak. Before you make this recipe, I suggest trying one of the soaked beans. It should have good crunch reminiscent of a fresh pod-pea. If it is chewy, drain them, fill them up with hot water again, and allow them to soak longer.
- Most falafel recipes have very similar ingredients. As it turns out, the trick is really in the method (how you process it) and in keeping the "dough" from becoming too wet. Because of this, I recommend not doing any ingredient substitutions. For a long time I was using fresh onion and fresh garlic, but the dough was too wet. When I went to dry onion and dry garlic, the dough was too dry, so I compromised with using fresh (refrigerated minced) garlic and dry onion. If you need to substitute, use one teaspoon dry garlic plus one teaspoon water. Do not substitute canned garbanzo beans—they will not have the same effect.
- I have two other recipes in this book that call for soaked garbanzo beans: The Best Hummus (page 170) and Easy Chickpea Snack (page 164). If you plan on making one of those at or around the same time as you are making this falafel, you can soak all the garbanzo beans at the same time and weigh out what you need for each recipe afterward. The formula you would use is this: 4 ounces dry garbanzo beans yields 8–9 ounces soaked beans.
- If you soak the beans and don't end up using them right away, you can keep them for up to a week in the fridge in water (change the water and rinse the beans once a day) or drained in a sealed container for a few days.

folded wraps

In Salt Lake City where I live, there used to be a wonderful chain called European Connection. They made fresh crepes and filled them will all kinds of fun sandwich and salad fillings. I recently encountered a similar stand (although not quite as high quality) in the Atlanta airport. In this recipe I give you ideas for the same type of yumminess I had at those places.

INSTRUCTIONS

1. Cook a ready-to-cook whole-grain tortilla. When you have turned it to the second side, add cheese in a thin layer on one half of the surface. Cook until the cheese softens or melts (depending on the type of cheese). As an alternative, you can buy or make crepes to use instead of tortillas. Many grocery stores (including Costco) sell premade crepes. If using premade crepes, warm and lightly crisp them on a griddle or in a pan before adding toppings.

2. Add other ingredients in the order listed below for the variation you are making. Fold the tortilla or crepe in quarters so that it is shaped like a cone. Open part of the "cone" and stuff it full of the greens and vegetables called for. Drizzle with dressing.

3. Eat immediately. These can be juicy, so have napkins on hand!

- **ITALIAN:** Sprinkle half the surface with a thin layer of shredded mozzarella. Add a sprinkle of Parmesan and a layer of fresh whole basil leaves. Fold. Stuff with diced tomato and baby spinach. Drizzle with a very small amount of mild Italian dressing.
- **APPLE AND BRIE:** Cut thin slices of Brie and very thin slices of apple. Melt the Brie, drizzle with balsamic glaze, and layer the apple on top of the Brie. Fold. Stuff with baby arugula and drizzle with a little more balsamic glaze.
- **BLT:** Sprinkle half the surface with goat cheese crumbles and tiny bits of precooked crispy bacon. Add thin sliced mushrooms or avocado. Fold. Stuff with tomato slices, finely sliced or diced red onion (optional), and baby spring greens. Drizzle with ranch dressing.
- **SCANDINAVIAN:** Mix ½–¾ teaspoon prepared horseradish, ⅛ teaspoon dill weed, ⅛ teaspoon agave (optional), and a dash of salt with ¼ cup Greek yogurt. Remove tortilla from heat and spread yogurt mixture on half the tortilla. Top with thin slices of smoked salmon (European style) or crumbles of cooked smoked salmon (Northwest US style). Fold. Stuff with cucumber, watercress, and baby spinach or frisée lettuce. If desired, drizzle with a little bit of honey mustard dressing or Classic French Vinaigrette (page 55).

TIPS

- The one I got in the Atlanta airport was handed to me in a paper cone like the ones used for snow cones. The paper cone helped contain the drips and worked great as a way to hold the wrap while I ate it.
- For ingredients like mushrooms and bacon, you can warm them up on the grill and then transfer them to the wrap.

garlic grilled green beans

These yummy and easy green beans still have a delightful crunch while having a cooked flavor. Give them a try as an appetizer or along with my Parmesan Zucchini and fresh garden tomatoes to make a meal.

INGREDIENTS	1X	2X
fresh green beans	6 oz.	12 oz.
olive oil	1 tsp.	2 tsp.
dry granulated garlic	½ tsp.	1 tsp.
As side dish serves:	1 to 2	2 to 4

INSTRUCTIONS

1. Wash and thoroughly dry the green beans.

2. Place the beans, oil, and garlic in a plastic bag and shake. Let sit at least 10 minutes.

3. Preheat an electric griddle to 400 degrees. Pour the beans onto the surface and spread out in a single layer. Cook on one side until the beans get dark brown "blisters" on that side (about 3 minutes). Then turn and cook the other side the same way.

4. Sprinkle lightly with salt before serving, if desired.

TIPS AND VARIATIONS

- Eat these beans hot off the grill, at room temperature, or cold.
- You can also make these beans in a hot frying pan or on a barbecue grill. If doing them on a grill, use a grilling basket and keep an eye on them so they don't burn!

grilled vegetable sandwich

Since I've been trying to boost the amount of vegetables I eat, I have tried several grilled vegetables sandwiches in restaurants and I'm always surprised how good they taste. This recipe combines elements of those restaurant sandwiches. Feel free to improvise and find what you like!

- **VEGETABLES:** This recipe works best with zucchini, eggplant, Portobello mushrooms, and red pepper. It doesn't matter too much how you cut these vegetables except they should be all about the same thickness. In this recipe I cut them all about ⅜-inch thick. You can also use red onion, roma tomatoes, soaked sun-dried tomatoes, or artichoke hearts. Cut onions a little thinner and tomatoes a little thicker so they will get done around the same time.
- **BREAD:** I like this best on slices of bread that have also been grilled or on toasted ciabatta rolls. You can grill the bread slices or roll halves as they are, or brush them lightly with olive oil.
- **TOPPINGS:** I recommend goat cheese with a sprinkle of granulated garlic and some baby arugula or baby spring greens.

INSTRUCTIONS

1. Wash and cut your vegetables. How many and what kind you do depends on how many you are serving and whether you want to have vegetables left over.
2. Dry the vegetables thoroughly and place them in a gallon zip-seal bag. Drizzle with olive oil and shake in some rosemary, basil, and granulated dry garlic. Add a very small amount of vinegar if desired (just a splash or two). Shake the bag to distribute your improvised vinaigrette. Let stand at least 10 minutes, or up to 24 hours in the fridge. If storing in the fridge, allow the vegetables to come back up to room temperature before grilling.
3. Preheat an electric griddle to 400 degrees. Place the vegetables on the griddle and roast on each side for 3–5 minutes.
4. Set vegetables aside and toast your bread or roll. Assemble your sandwich using the vegetables and toppings of your choice or present the vegetables and toppings and allow each person to assemble his or her own hot sandwich. If the sandwiches cool off while they are being assembled, put the completed sandwiches back on the griddle to warm up again.

TIPS

- These can be done on a gas outdoor grill if you prefer. You will need to carefully monitor the veggies so they don't burn. You can also do them in a George Foreman style grill. Arrange the veggies on the grill, close the grill, and cook 5–7 minutes.
- Instead of using Portobello mushrooms, you can use finely sliced regular mushrooms. To do this, sauté them separately, then add them as a topping in step four.

- Leftover vegetables keep fine in the fridge and taste good cold as well as hot. You can also freeze them to use another time. A traditional Italian salad serves finely cut, hot grilled veggies on a bed of greens. This would be a great way to use leftover veggies.

nancy's fish tacos

This is a recipe where the fish eaters can enjoy the fish, but there are still plenty of other yummy food to fill up the shell for those who don't.

INGREDIENTS	1X	2X
frozen or fresh fish fillets—any kind of white fish (uncooked weight)	7–9 oz.	14–18 oz.
finely shredded cabbage	about 7 oz. or half of a 14-ounce bag	about 14 oz. or 1 (14-oz.) bag
Guacamole (see page 168)	1x recipe	2x recipe
Pico de Gallo (see page 166)	1x recipe or 8 oz. store-bought	2x recipe or 16 oz. store-bought
fresh cilantro	about ½ a bunch	1 bunch
whole-grain ready-to-cook tortillas	about 4	about 8
Serves:	2	4

INSTRUCTIONS

1. Arrange fish on a lined baking sheet and sprinkle generously with dry granulated onion and a little cayenne pepper. You can also use salt and pepper. Bake at 425 degrees for about 10 minutes or until fish flakes easily with a fork.
2. Prepare the Guacamole and Pico de Gallo.
3. Wash the cilantro and snip into pieces.
4. Cook the tortillas when everything else is ready.
5. Assemble the tacos as desired with fish, cabbage, cilantro, guacamole, and pico. Top with Michele's Lime-Cilantro Dressing (see page 178) or other southwest dressing of your choice.

TIPS AND VARIATIONS

- For gluten-free tacos, use gluten-free wraps or corn tortillas.
- You can also present this as a salad: fill bowl with greens, add a layer of cabbage, and dollops of guacamole. Drizzle with dressing and add small pieces of fish.
- We have tried this recipe using frozen tempura shrimp instead of the fish. It was very crunchy and very tasty. We used the spicy fruit sauce that came with the shrimp instead of the pico de gallo and dressing.

parmesan zucchini

Zucchini, like all squash, was a New World food that was brought back to Europe by explorers several hundred years ago. The varieties of squash we know as zucchini arrived in the United States by way of Italy. In other parts of the world, zucchini is known as courgette or marrows. Whatever you call it, zucchini, and its close relative the yellow summer squash, can be fun to cook with! This recipe is my favorite way to eat them.

INGREDIENTS

young zucchini or yellow summer squash

butter or olive oil

shredded Parmesan or Romano cheese

INSTRUCTIONS

1. Cut slices of zucchini or yellow summer squash about ¼-inch thick. Place them on a electric griddle preheated to 350 degrees and coated lightly with butter or olive oil. Cook for 3–5 minutes or until underneath side is starting to brown.

2. Turn each piece and sprinkle with shredded Parmesan or Romano cheese. Cook on the second side for 2–3 minutes or until the cheese melts. Tastes best warm but can also be served cold.

TIPS AND VARIATIONS

- If you don't have an electric griddle you can pan-fry on medium high or bake at 375 degrees.
- While Parmesan is the cheese we hear about the most, I prefer using Romano or a Parmesan-Romano blend. Try Parmesan and Romano side by side sometime and decide which you like better.
- You can use Parmesan Zucchini instead of slices of mozzarella to make a Caprese salad. Just layer it with fresh sliced tomatoes then drizzle with a little balsamic glaze and add fresh basil. It can be served on a bed of arugula.
- For variety, you can sprinkle the squash with dry granulated onion before adding the Parmesan or Romano cheese. Or, for a pizza effect, use granulated dry garlic, a little dry oregano, and basil (crumble them in your fingers as you sprinkle them) on the squash just before you add the cheese.

puréed parsnips

Parsnips look like carrots but are cream-colored. When I was young, my mom used to make parsnips occasionally as a vegetable with dinner. She would cut them like carrot strips, steam them, and then pan-fry them in butter. I remember feeling quite suspicious of them the first time I had them. My mom explained that they had a mellow flavor and would taste good because of having been browned in butter. I tried them and liked them! I didn't love the stringy texture, but I did love the mellow creamy flavor, which was enhanced by the butter. In this recipe, you don't have to worry about the texture and can just enjoy the wonderful mellow flavor.

INGREDIENTS	PER POUND
parsnips	1 lb
water	to cover
salt for the water	½ tsp
cooking liquid	5–6 Tbsp.
butter	1 Tbsp.
ground nutmeg	¼ tsp.
black pepper	as desired
Serves (as side dish):	3 to 4

INSTRUCTIONS

1. Peel the parsnips and trim the ends. Cut in 1-inch pieces.

2. Place the pieces in a pot and add water to cover. Bring to a boil.

3. Add the salt, cover, and reduce heat to a low simmer. Cook until the parsnips are very tender—about 25–30 minutes.

4. Drain the cooking water into a measuring container. Transfer the parsnips to a food processor. Process until they start to get very thick. Add half of the cooking liquid called for in the recipe, the butter, and the seasonings. Process until very smooth and creamy, with a mashed potato–like consistency. Add more of the cooking liquid called for if they seem too sticky.

TIPS AND VARIATIONS

- Vegetable purées of this type are appearing more and more in high-end restaurants. Often this kind of purée will be served under seafood. I have seen pan-fried sea scallops served over a parsnip purée or over sunchoke purée (delicious!). Celery root also works very well.
- In this recipe the nutmeg doesn't stand out. It just underscores and mellows the flavor of the parsnips like bay leaf does in my Artichokes recipe.
- You can make a delicious creamy soup from this purée by adding some broth (flavor of your choice) and some half and half. Garnish with finely chopped fresh Italian parsley.

pad thai

I wasn't really a fan of pad Thai until my niece Elaine made it one night when I was visiting. This recipe is very similar to hers, but uses more bean sprouts and fewer noodles. Interestingly, as long as there are some noodles in the recipe, the lightly-cooked bean sprouts come across as if they were noodles.

INGREDIENTS	1X
pad Thai brown rice noodles	4 oz.
green onions—white part	5
green onions—green part	5
mini red or yellow bell peppers	3-4 (about 3 oz.)
mung bean sprouts	12–14 oz.
fresh cilantro	½ bunch (1–1½ oz.)
fresh lime	1 whole
roasted peanuts	¼–½ cup (1–2 oz.)
coconut oil	1 Tbsp.
minced garlic (fridge)	2 tsp.
eggs	2
pad Thai sauce	4 oz. (half of 8-oz. jar)
pan size:	12-inch skillet or large wok
Feeds:	Feeds: 2

INSTRUCTIONS

PART I:

1. Place the noodles in a container of hot water to soak. They will need about 30 minutes to soak which should be about the amount of time you will need to prep the produce.

2. Prepare all the vegetables: finely slice the white parts of the green onions; snip the green parts of the green onions into ¼ to ½-inch pieces and place in a separate container; remove seeds and finely slice the peppers; rinse the mung bean sprouts; wash and roughly chop the cilantro (leaf part only); cut the lime in half. Cut one of the halves into wedges.

3. Chop the peanuts and set aside.

PART II:

1. Melt the coconut oil in a 12-inch skillet or wok over medium high heat. When the pan is hot, add the garlic and white parts of the green onion. Add the eggs and scramble them. Remove pan from heat. Stir the pad Thai sauce in with the eggs and squeeze in the juice from the half of lime.

2. Check the noodles. They should be *al dente* or nearly as soft as you want them for eating. If they are not soft enough, drain and place them in hot water for an additional 5–10 minutes.

3. When the noodles are ready, drain them and add them to the pan, stirring them together with the sauce and egg mixture.

PART III:

1. When you are ready with all the vegetables, return the pan to the heat with the heat on high. Once the pan is hot again, add the chopped peppers, bean sprouts, about half of the green onion, half of the cilantro, and half the chopped nuts. Stir while cooking until the ingredients are combined and the bean sprouts are becoming limp.

2. Remove from heat and stir in the remaining green onion and cilantro. Garnish with remaining chopped nuts and serve. Offer lime wedges on the side.

TIPS

- I like to use Annie Chun brand noodles and the Thai Kitchen brand sauce that comes in 8-oz. jars. It is possible to make you own Pad Thai sauce, but it is complicated and takes specialty ingredients that are hard to find. You can find Pad Thai sauce in jars online, in most grocery stores, or in Asian markets.
- When the noodles are ready, but still in the water, I take kitchen shears and cut them into slightly smaller pieces. This makes the finished Pad Thai a little easier to eat.
- This recipe feeds two hungry adults. If you need to feed more people, you will need to use two frying pans or do more than one batch. If you need to do a double or triple batch, one option is to do Part II, Step 1 for all the batches at the same time, and then transfer the egg-sauce mixture to another container. When your vegetables are prepped, heat your pan, place the portion of noodles and vegetables that you need for one batch in the pan, and add the portion of the egg mixture you need. Stir-fry over high heat. This only takes a couple minutes; then you can do the same with the next batches.
- You can do Parts I and II ahead of time and then refrigerate or freeze the "base"—the noodles, eggs, and sauce. Place the prepared peppers, bean sprouts, green onions, and chopped cilantro in a sealed plastic bag and refrigerate for up to 24 or even 48 hours. When you are ready to cook, put the "base" back in the pan and do Part III. Part III can also be done in a microwave. Having all this ready ahead of time makes it easier to prepare for a larger group since you can do Part III of one batch and then immediately do Part III of a second or third batch.
- Leftovers of this recipe taste great. Just reheat gently in the microwave or in a skillet.

savory onions

Nearly every Sunday when I was growing up, my mom made pot roast—roast beef surrounded by potatoes, carrots, and onions—in her big cast iron Dutch oven. One of my dad's favorite parts was the roasted onions. Roasted onions are very high in umami*—the savory flavor we often associate with meat. Roasting boosts the savory flavor of most vegetables, but none will smell as delicious as these.*

INGREDIENTS

4–5 yellow onions

olive oil or meted butter

salt

INSTRUCTIONS

1. Trim the smallest amount you can off the root end of the onions. Cut off the stem end and then cut each onion into eighths through the root, making sure that each section has a little root so it will stay together. Remove the outer two layers from each section.

2. Arrange the onion sections on a lined baking sheet. Brush each with olive oil or melted butter, and sprinkle lightly with salt.

3. Bake at 400 degrees for 30–40 minutes, depending on desired doneness. Serve them on top of Zucchini Spaghetti, on a roasted vegetable sandwich, or as a side dish with other vegetables. Or freeze them to use to boost the flavor in recipes that call for sautéed onions like my Huevos Rancheros or Vegetarian Chili. Makes about 1 cup of roasted onions.

TIPS AND VARIATIONS

- Instead of salt, you can drizzle the onions lightly with soy sauce to increase the *umami* even more.
- At Thanksgiving time, if I roast a turkey I will save some of the drippings to use instead of olive oil or butter in this recipe.
- Oven roasted vegetables are very popular right now. Do a search on almost any vegetable "roasted" and you will find lots of delicious recipes that use a similar method to this roasted onion recipe.

sharla's easy minestrone

I had this at Sharla's house one day when I dropped by and she offered to feed me. That was more than five years ago and I still remember that soup! Sharla says she likes to make it because it is a soup her whole family loves.

INGREDIENTS	1X
whole carrots	4–5 (about 2 cups diced)
yellow onion	¼–½ onion
celery stalks	3 stalks (about 1 cup diced)
olive oil	1 Tbsp.
petite diced tomatoes	1 (15-oz.) can
tomato sauce	1 (8-oz.) can
kidney beans	1 (15-oz.) can
white beans	1 (15-oz.) can
water	7 cups
beef or vegetable base (see Tip)	1 Tbsp.
dry basil leaf	1–2 tsp.
dry granulated onion	¼ tsp.
dry granulated garlic	⅛–¼ tsp.
small dry pasta of choice (like shells)	4–8 oz.
green beans	1 (15-oz.) can
Makes:	about 15 cups

INSTRUCTIONS

1. Peel and dice the carrots. Dice the onion and celery. Heat the olive oil in a pot that will hold the finished soup. Sauté the vegetables over medium-high heat until the onion starts to look translucent.

2. Add the tomatoes and tomato sauce. Drain and rinse the kidney and white beans and add to the pot.

3. Add the water, broth base and seasonings. Bring to a boil, then reduce heat and simmer 15–45 minutes.

4. About 20 minutes before you want to eat, add the pasta. When it is tender, drain the green beans and add them.

SERVE with Parmesan cheese on top.

TIPS

- Exact amounts aren't critical for the vegetables in this soup.
- For the other soups in this section, I prefer vegetable broth not from concentrate. For this recipe, it is easier to adjust the soup using refrigerated broth concentrate (like Better than Boullion brand).

swiss chard—spanakopita style

My parents always grew Swiss chard in their garden when I was growing up. One evening after dinner when I was about ten, my mom came into the living room and sadly announced she had forgotten to serve the chard she had planned for dinner. She had it all ready to go in a pot but hadn't turned it on. We all said we would be willing to try and eat some, so she went ahead and cooked it. I got to eat it in the living room with butter melted on it and sprinkled with cider vinegar. Eating it by itself like that I really explored the texture and flavor and decided I liked it. Since then I enjoy eating Swiss chard alone or as part of a meal.

INGREDIENTS	1X	2X
Swiss chard or other greens	8–10 oz.	16-20 oz.
dry granulated onion	1 tsp.	2 tsp.
dry dill weed	½–1 tsp.	1–2 tsp.
water	½ cup	1 cup
balsamic vinegar	1 tsp.	2 tsp.
crumbled goat cheese	2–4 Tbsp.	¼–½ cup
Serves (as side dish):	1	2

INSTRUCTIONS

1. Submerge the leaves in clean water and "slosh" them around to remove any sand. Let them drain in a colander. Change the water and repeat if desired.

2. Lay a pile of 10–12 leaves on a cutting board and slice them into 1- to 2-inch wide strips. You can do this using a chef's knife or large serrated knife.

3. Place the chard in a large frying pan with a lid. (The chard will cook down quite a bit, so it doesn't matter if it is mounded up in the pan as long as you can get the lid on. If you are cooking a larger batch, you will need to use a large pot instead of a frying pan.)

4. Add the water, granulated onion, and dill. Put the lid on and turn on to high. When steam starts to escape, reduce the heat to medium high.

5. When the water has evaporated and the chard is dark green, glossy, and taking up much less space, transfer it to a serving bowl.

6. Toss quickly with the vinegar and goat cheese, and serve.

TIPS AND VARIATIONS

- You can chop the stems and include them in the recipe or keep them to eat raw or use in a stir-fry. Eaten raw, they are similar to celery in texture but with a slightly "salty" flavor.
- You can use this same recipe to cook any large leafy green that isn't too tough. All of these greens tend to be a little sandy, so submerging them to wash them is critical if you don't want them to taste "gritty."
- Alternate version: use apple cider vinegar instead of balsamic, and dot with butter instead of using goat cheese. Very simple, yet delicious—my favorite way to have it.

tom's cabbage borscht

In the United States, we think of borscht as a red beet soup, often served cold. In eastern Europe, though, there are as many different kinds of borscht as there are types of chili in the States and they are usually served hot. While all (or nearly all) have beets, some have more cabbage than beets and are not as red. My nephew Tom spent some time living in Ukraine and learned to make several different versions of this hearty vegetable soup. What I love about this borscht is the way the cooked cabbage becomes so mellow as it cooks with the other vegetables and makes the soup so satisfying and filling. This recipe makes a large batch, but it's something that works well as leftovers. It's a nice thing to come home to in the winter!

INGREDIENTS	1X	2X
vegetable stock (see Tip)	7 cups	14 cups
medium fresh beets	1 beet	2 beets
medium potatoes	1 potato	2 potatoes
shredded cabbage	half a medium head or 10–12 oz.	1 medium head or 20–24 oz.
matchstick carrots (optional)	1½ oz.	3 oz.
olive oil	2 tsp.	4 tsp.
medium yellow onion	1 onion or about 8 oz.	2 onions or about 16 oz.
minced garlic (fridge)	1–2 tsp.	2–4 tsp.
dry dill weed	3 Tbsp.	6 Tbsp.
Makes:	2½ quarts	5 quarts
Serves:	4 to 5	8 to 10

INSTRUCTIONS

1. Bring the vegetable stock to a boil in an appropriate size pot for the batch you are doing. Meanwhile, peel the beet (a potato peeler works fine for this) and finely shred it or chop it (this is easiest to do in a food processor). Use a ceramic or glass plate when cutting your beet—beet juice can stain plastic and will also stain your hands for a few minutes.

2. Add the beets to the boiling broth and allow to cook for about ten minutes while you complete the rest of this step. Preheat the olive oil in a sauté pan. Finely chop the onion and start it cooking on medium-high heat in the sauté pan. Peel the potato and dice into ⅜-inch cubes.

3. Add the diced potato to the boiling broth. When the onion is lightly brown, add the garlic and sauté briefly. Shred the cabbage. Add the onion-garlic mixture, the

cabbage, and the carrot (if using) to the soup. Bring to a boil over high heat.

4. Once the soup comes to a boil, reduce the heat so that the soup will stay at a low simmer. Add half the dill and cover the pot. Simmer for at least one hour and up to 2½ hours.

5. Stir in the other half of the dill just before serving. Serve hot with a dollop of sour cream.

TIPS AND VARIATIONS

- Whenever you cook any vegetable from the cabbage family, it's likely to taste great but smell a little funny while it is cooking. The dill in this recipe helps mask that smell.
- My current favorite vegetable stock is Full Circle brand, which comes in 1-quart cartons.
- Depending on the brand of vegetable stock you use you may need to add some salt and pepper at the end. You can instead use vegetable stock concentrate (that comes as a paste in a glass jar) but should start with about half as much as the directions on the jar and add more if you need it after the soup is put together.
- For convenience you can use a 14-oz. bag of coleslaw mix (containing cabbage and carrots) instead of the cabbage and carrots in the recipe or use a 10-oz. or 12-oz. bag of shredded cabbage and matchstick carrots (or no carrots). If you are using whole cabbage, buy a head that weighs around 2 pounds.

veggie fajitas

I originally experimented with fajitas years ago because I loved cooking them outdoors in a cast iron camp oven. I included a version of this recipe in my first book, Dutch Oven Cookout: Step-by-Step. *It is a recipe that can be done vegetarian or with meat, indoors or out!*

INGREDIENTS	1X	2X
yellow onions	2 medium size	4 medium size
red or yellow bell peppers	2 medium size	4 medium size
small tomatoes	2	4
minced garlic (fridge)	1 tsp.	2 tsp.
black pepper	½ tsp.	1 tsp.
soy sauce or shoyu	2–4 Tbsp.	¼–½ cup
fresh lime juice	2–3 Tbsp.	4–6 Tbsp.
tortillas	4–6 tortillas	8–12 tortillas
sauté pan size	10 inch	14 inch
serves:	2 to 4	4 to 8

INSTRUCTIONS

1. Cut the onions in half and then in slices. Prepare the peppers in strips. Dice the tomatoes (can also roughly chop in a food processor).

2. Put all the vegetables in a bag and add the garlic, black pepper, soy sauce, and the fresh squeezed lime juice. Shake together to mix. Seal the bag and allow to sit for ten to twenty minutes.

3. Preheat a little oil in a heavy-bottomed sauté pan, cast-iron skillet or a wok. When the pan is hot, dump in the vegetables and sauté or stir-fry over high heat so that the liquid becomes a glaze. Keep the heat high enough that the vegetable juices evaporate as they cook. Only stir-fry the vegetables long enough to be warmed through.

4. Serve on tortillas with Guacamole (page 168), Pico de Gallo (page 166), and fresh cilantro.

TIPS

- It's important to have a big enough pan for your batch size and have the pan really hot before starting, otherwise you will end up with too much liquid. In this recipe the juices from the vegetables should evaporate as it cooks.
- I like to use refrigerated uncooked tortillas for this and cook them just before serving. If using pre-cooked tortillas, warm them up before adding the toppings.
- You can make this recipe using chicken or beef strips. Reduce the onion, peppers, and tomato by half, and use half a pound of meat for the 1x recipe. If desired, place the meat and the marinade ingredients in a bag the night before you want to make it. Refrigerate until ready to cook. Add the vegetables to the marinade/meat combination just before cooking.
- For videos showing how to cook this outdoors in a cast iron Dutch oven, see my outdoor cooking website: www.DutchOvenCookout.com.

yummy broccoli

I'm one of those people who tends to avoid the broccoli on a veggie tray (even now . . .) but when I first had this I couldn't get enough. It was my niece who introduced me to it, and I couldn't believe how simple the recipe was. I also couldn't believe how excited her kids were that she was making it! This recipe also tastes great raw. As I said before, I'm not a fan of broccoli on a veggie tray, but I like it this way either cooked or raw. Raw, it reminds me a little bit of eating movie theater popcorn. And it looks very pretty because the oil gives it a brighter color.

INGREDIENTS	1X	3X
broccoli florets	1 pound	3 pounds
olive oil	1–2½ Tbsp.	3–7½ Tbsp.
salt	¼–½ tsp.	¾–1½ tsp.
baking pan	9 x 9	half sheet (13 x 18)
Serves:	2	6

INSTRUCTIONS

1. Toss florets with olive oil and salt until all surfaces of the vegetables are coated. Recipe works best if all the florets are around the same size.

2. Pour onto a baking sheet. You can use parchment or a reusable pan liner if desired.

3. Bake at 425 degrees for 10 to 15 minutes—how long it takes will depend on your oven. The broccoli should be starting to brown on the tips but still be chewy. Do not use convection.

TIPS AND VARIATIONS

- Another way to do this: leave out the salt and sprinkle the vegetables with shredded Parmesan or Romano cheese a few minutes before it is done—just long enough for the cheese to melt.
- When I first made this recipe I had the oven on convection. I kept checking it, but suddenly the florets were all brown to dark brown. I thought I was going to have to throw it away—it looked like it would taste awful—but then I tried it and it was good, more like a slight caramel flavor rather than a burnt flavor.
- The 3x recipe calls for three pounds because that is how much is in the large bag of florets Costco sells. It also happens to fit just right in a half sheet pan (commonly known as a jelly roll pan.) Pre-cut florets are easier, but fresh broccoli on the stalk generally has better flavor. If you buy it in a bag as florets, be sure to use it within a day or two of when you buy it.
- You can also do this recipe with cauliflower but may need less oil.
- Do an online search for variations of this basic recipe! Roasted vegetable recipes are very popular.

zucchini spaghetti

I became convinced that it was worth buying a spiralizer to make zucchini noodles after reading my cousin's comment that her little girls loved zucchini spaghetti and would ask for it specifically. It's become my second-favorite way to eat zucchini!

INGREDIENTS	1X
grocery store size zucchini or yellow squash	1 medium squash, 12–14 oz.
olive oil	1–1 ½ Tbsp.
dry granulated onion	¼–½ tsp.
dry leaf basil (optional)	¼–½ tsp.
shredded Parmesan cheese	2–4 Tbsp.
spaghetti sauce (your choice)	¾–1 cup
Serves:	1 adult

INSTRUCTIONS

1. Cut off one end of your zucchini and secure it in your spiralizer. Crank until the squash has been cut into "noodles." You may need to pick out some mushy seeds if you are using a larger squash. Use scissors to cut down through the zucchini "noodles" a few times so that they are in nice lengths (not one long spiral).

2. Toss the "noodles" with the olive oil, dry onion, and dry basil in a microwaveable bowl. The onion and basil don't strongly affect the end flavor, but seem to make the overall dish taste more like spaghetti. Do not add salt or the zucchini will start to release water or "weep."

3. Microwave 2–4 minutes (depending on amount you are making and on your microwave) or until the noodles are just barely hot. Heating them just enough preserves the nutrients and it gives them the slightly "floppy" noodle texture you want for this dish. If you cook them too long, they will become mushy.

4. Toss with Parmesan or Romano cheese or Italian cheese blend and serve, or serve into individual dishes and top with your favorite sauce. If topping with sauce, serve the sauce hot so that it doesn't cool down the noodles.

TIPS AND VARIATIONS

- As long as your "noodles" are not exposed to salt, they shouldn't "weep" or become watery. If you toss them with sauce that contains salt and then let them sit, they will become watery. If this happens, you can just drain off the liquid and add a little more sauce.
- I like to run some red or sweet white onion through my spiralizer, and add it to the "spaghetti." I do this even when I'm using sauce because I think it enhances the overall flavor. I usually use about ¼ onion per adult serving
- If you have a garden, or know someone who does, chances are that you may have access to free zucchini that has gotten a little bit too big. This can be fun way to eat that slightly overgrown zucchini. (Zucchini that is really huge doesn't turn well in my spiralizer, but medium-large works great.)
- I am always hesitant to recommend a recipe that can only be made using a specialty piece of equipment. Not only is it another expense, but you end up having to find a place to store the equipment once you have it. That being said, I don't have any regrets that I bought a spiralizer. I think it has paid for itself in a couple of years (especially considering that in the summer, at least where I live, zucchini is pretty much free). There is a certain fun factor to what I can do with this gadget that I think makes it worth having. If you decide to get one you can easily compare brands and read reviews by looking up "spiralizer" online.
- If you have never tried growing zucchini, it is quite easy to grow in many climates and tends to produce prolifically. You can plant one in a flower bed or balcony planter box.

A FEW MORE IDEAS FROM AROUND THE WORLD

In the United States, it is typical to have one vegetable with a meal (or none) - whether at home, or eating out. I have found it interesting in my travels to see multiple vegetables and salads served at the same time, for the same meal. Below are some examples.

This colorful and delicious array of cooked vegetables was served at a 50th Anniversary celebration I attended in Germany. The vegetables in the photo are: steamed broccoli, baby carrots, green beans, white asparagus with Hollandaise sauce, green peas, and cauliflower with Hollandaise sauce. Hollandaise sauce makes any cooked vegetable taste special. At home when I serve vegetables like this for a group I like to use the refrigerated Hollandaise sauce from Trader Joe's, or else make a sauce like the one on page 99.

In Italy, my brother-in-law ordered a cooked fish and it came with this beautiful plate of lightly cooked/grilled vegetables served cold. They were pretty to look at and very tasty! (In France a similar plate might be referred to as crudites.) You can make a variety plate like this using my Grilled Vegetable Sandwich recipe on page 112 or by lightly cooking and chilling other vegetables like the carrot slices and cauliflower florets in the photo.

In Brazil, most buffets serve a huge variety of cold and hot vegetable dishes. You can get some idea of this by visiting a salad bar at a Brazilian grill in the U.S. When I visit a buffet like this, I'm really not even tempted by the heavier dishes because there are so many fun salads and vegetables to try. Do an image search online on "Brazilian salads" to find more fun recipes similar to my Brazilian Heart of Palm Salad recipe on page 49.

FREQUENTLY ASKED QUESTIONS

YOU USE BUTTER IN QUITE A FEW OF YOUR COOKED VEGETABLE RECIPES, BUT I DON'T LIKE BUTTER. CAN I SUBSTITUTE SOMETHING ELSE?

If you grew up during the '70s or '80s or in a family that used mostly margarine, it's quite possible you never got used to the flavor of butter. If you still use margarine, I think it's a good idea to get used to high quality butter or olive oil instead. Butter and olive oil have been around for millennia, margarine for less than a century. There is evidence that the oils used in margarine can cause inflammation in the body. While the evidence is still young, I think it is worth thinking about.

If you grew up eating mostly lightly steamed vegetables with little or no butter, oil, or margarine of any kind, and you think you don't like vegetables, I suggest giving them another try using some of my recipes. Vegetables that are cooked to tender and have a little fat or salt can taste really good and often come across as an entirely different vegetable. To learn more about butter, see page 154 and page 181.

YOU TALK QUITE A BIT ABOUT NUTRIENTS, BUT I'M NOT SURE I UNDERSTAND HOW YOU USE THE TERM. WHAT DO YOU MEAN WHEN YOU SAY SOMETHING HAS MORE "NUTRIENTS"?

The word *nutrient* has been evolving in its usage over the past hundred years. Over a hundred and twenty years ago, when fats, proteins, and carbohydrates were first discovered, the word *nutrient* referred to them as a group. In the 1920s, when research revealed the existence of vitamins, the definition had to be expanded. Currently nutrition science talks about "macronutrients" and "micronutrients." In human nutrition, macronutrients are the proteins, fats, and carbs. Micronutrients are the vitamins, minerals, antioxidants, and a whole host of other things that are still being discovered. In modern everyday usage, when people talk about "nutrients," they are usually referring to micronutrients and that is how I use the term in this book.

WHEN YOU SAY SOME FOOD HAS MORE NUTRIENTS THAN ANOTHER FOOD, ISN'T THAT IRRELEVANT? CAN'T I JUST TAKE A SUPPLEMENT AND THEN NOT WORRY ABOUT WHAT I EAT?

As research into vitamins, minerals, and micronutrients progresses, science keeps finding new and smaller particles in natural foods that influence how the body functions. I think it would be very unwise to assume that we currently know everything there is to know about antioxidants, bioflavinoids, and other things for which we don't yet have names. As I mentioned in the previous FAQ, a hundred years ago, basic knowledge of vitamins was just dawning. Scientific study of human health and nutrition moves slowly (or at least it does when done well). Until we know much more than we currently do, I think the safest way to get our bodies the needed micronutrients is to eat lots of greens and vegetables.

SECTION 4

Weekend Breakfasts and Healthy Breads

- OF DISNEYLAND AND DUTCH OVENS
- RECIPES

OF DISNEYLAND AND DUTCH OVENS

My husband and I are Disneyland fans. We don't have any kids, so, except for when we go with nieces and nephews, Disneyland for us is an easy way to get away from the cold for a few days, spend time with each other, and get some sun. A few years ago we ended up getting an annual pass and had enough opportunities to go that we were no longer in a hurry to get to the attractions. Instead we were content to enjoy the atmosphere, people watch, and … eat! It may surprise you to know that Disneyland serves a lot of quite healthy food. Several recipes in this book were influenced by things I tried there, and two of the recipes in this section were directly inspired by menu items from the Carnation Cafe on Main Street, USA. We both used to really look forward to eating the Huevos Rancheros and the Oatmeal Cakes with Fruit Compote served there … until they were taken off the menu. My versions aren't identical, but they are still really tasty.

Another big part of my life is Dutch oven cooking. I worked for many years at a local girls camp and every year I was involved in planning and preparing for the meals the campers would cook with charcoal in cast-iron camp ovens. There were so many times (at the start) that these outdoor meals didn't turn out, that I eventually came up with an essentially foolproof cookout method, which became my first book, *Dutch Oven Cookout: Step-by-Step*. Dutch oven cooking doesn't have a lot in common with salads and green smoothies (although you can definitely cook some tasty vegetables that way!). But there was one cast-iron recipe I felt had to go in here: my no-knead bread. In terms of nutrients, breads in general are significantly below vegetables and greens; however, a really good slice of homemade bread can make one's enjoyment of a salad so much greater! My no-knead bread recipe is even easier than other no-knead recipes you can read about online. The steps are mix, rise, dump, and bake … and it comes out like a crusty loaf of mild sourdough.

While smoothies are my favorite breakfast because they are so fast, easy, portable, and nutritious, sometimes I feel like I want something else instead. When we were getting started with green smoothies and our bodies were adjusting to the extra greens, we generally had some version of the Buckwheat Muesli every second or third day and had my Puffy Whole-Grain Pancakes on the weekend. We still like to make the pancakes, but now we generally just freeze them and toast one to eat with a smoothie. When we have time on the weekend, our special treat now is Huevos Rancheros—yum!

FYI, most of the recipes in this section are, or can be, vegan and several are gluten-free (like most of the other recipes in this book). One thing we like to do is have friends over for breakfast. We offer them some green smoothie and make one of the breakfasts in this chapter. It can be a great way to introduce people to Eating and Drinking Green.

oatmeal cakes with fruit sauce

I first had something like this at a restaurant in Disneyland. Since the Carnation Café no longer serves these, I had to come up with my own version. This is a delicious and festive recipe for winter or summer.

INGREDIENTS	1X	2X
quick rolled oats	1 cup (3¾ oz.)	2 cups (7½ oz.)
chia or ground chia	2 Tbsp.	¼ cup
almond flour or other flour	¼ cup	½ cup
cinnamon	1–2 tsp.	2–4 tsp.
cloves	⅛-¼ tsp.	¼–½ tsp.
salt	⅛-¼ tsp	¼–½ tsp.
water	6 Tbsp. (3 oz.)	¾ cup (6 oz..)
real maple syrup	2 Tbsp. (1 oz.)	¼ cup (2 oz.)
vanilla extract	1 tsp.	2 tsp.
coconut oil	1½–2 Tbsp. (¾–1 oz.)	3–4 Tbsp. (1½–2 oz.)
Serves:	2 to 3	4 to 6

INSTRUCTIONS

1. Combine the dry ingredients.

2. Heat the water to boiling and add the maple syrup, vanilla and coconut oil. Stir until the oil melts. Mix with the dry ingredients.

3. Cover and let stand overnight or for at least one hour. When ready to cook, scoop the mixture and form into one-ounce patties about ½-inch thick by 2- to 3-inches wide. Cook at 350 degrees on a lightly buttered electric griddle or in a frying pan on medium-high heat until lightly browned on each side—about 5 minutes per side.

4. Serve warm with fruit sauce (recipe follows.) Garnish with fresh berries if desired.

TIPS AND VARIATIONS

- Choose your cinnamon and cloves amounts depending on how cinnamony you like things.
- You can substitute the same weight of Scottish oatmeal (Bob's Red Mill brand or similar—not the same as steel-cut oats) for the rolled oats: 3¾ ounces of Scottish oatmeal is ⅔ cup.
- If your cook time is shorter than 5 minutes per side, turn down your heat so that the oatmeal cakes have time to get done in the middle.
- This recipe can be used to make granola. Spread the dough half an inch thick on a lined baking sheet. Bake at 350 for 25–30 minutes or until the edges start to brown. Remove from oven and turn over the granola in sections with a spatula. Leave on pan to cool. Granola should be crunchy or just slightly chewy after it cools.

FRUIT SAUCE

This fruit sauce recipe is essentially the same as the fruit smoothie recipe on page 186. The main difference is that you don't purée the second type of fruit you add. Just like with my Great Fruit Smoothie recipe, you can use any combination of fruit. I like the tartness of this raspberry-orange-cranberry version with the warm spices in the Oatmeal Cakes, but you can try any combination.

INGREDIENTS	1X	2X
orange juice	1–2 oz.	2–4 oz.
fresh orange, peeled	2 oz. (½ medium orange)	4 oz. (1 medium orange)
cranberries (fresh or thawed)	3 oz.	6 oz. (half a bag)
agave	½ Tbsp.	1 Tbsp.
coconut oil	¾–1 Tbsp. (⅜–½ oz.)	1½–2 Tbsp. (¾–1 oz.)
frozen raspberries	3 oz.	6 oz.
Makes:	10 oz.	20 oz.

INSTRUCTIONS

1. Place the orange juice, peeled orange, fresh or thawed cranberries, agave, and coconut oil in blender. Process on high until smooth, creamy and all one color. There should be no chunks of coconut oil.

2. Add the frozen raspberries and pulse until just barely combined (the raspberries should be broken up but not puréed).

3. Serve over hot Oatmeal Cakes. Plan on 3–5 ounces fruit sauce per person.

TIPS

- In a high-power blender, you should have no problem getting the coconut oil to blend in with the fruit. In a regular blender with sharp blades, you may need to melt the coconut oil before adding it or else heat up the orange juice.
- The orange juice is in the recipe mainly because most blenders need a little liquid to get started. If you would like your sauce to be thicker, you can reduce or leave out the orange juice (as long as your sauce will still blend).
- Eat leftover sauce as a cold fruit pudding or fruit smoothie, or freeze to use another time. You can freeze it in an ice cube tray and use a cube or two with reheated oatmeal cakes.

buckwheat muesli

When my husband and I started drinking intensely green smoothies, we both found our bodies weren't up to handling that many greens every day at first, so we alternated with this yummy and nutritious muesli. It is soaked, not cooked, so it doesn't take any cooking time in the morning.

INGREDIENTS	1X	2X
raw buckwheat groats	4 oz. (~½ cup)	8 oz. (~1 cup)
chopped raw almonds or pecans	½ oz. (a few nuts)	1 oz. (a small handful)
craisins	¾ oz. (a small handful)	1½ oz. (a handful)
cinnamon stick	1	1
water for soaking	1½ cups	3 cups
orange	1–1 ½	3 whole
apple(s)	1	2
applesauce	About ¾ cup	about 1½ cups
kefir or plain yogurt	about ¼ cup	about ½ cup
Serves:	2	4

INSTRUCTIONS

1. Mix together the buckwheat, chopped nuts, craisins, and cinnamon. Add water and leave to soak overnight.

2. In the morning, transfer the mixture to a colander to drain, and then rinse with fresh water. Remove the cinnamon stick. (You can rinse it, let it dry, and use it again one to two more times.) Transfer the muesli to a bowl.

3. Peel the orange and cut it and the apple into bite-size pieces. Add the fruit, the applesauce, and the kefir to the soaked mixture. Add a sprinkle of cinnamon and a dash of cloves. Mix and serve.

TIPS AND VARIATIONS

- Buckwheat is a seed, not a grain and not related to wheat.
- *Muesli* is a Swiss term. It originally referred to a mixture of oats and yogurt that were soaked overnight and then mixed with fresh cut fruit in the morning.
- Tropical Muesli variation: leave out the nuts, craisins, and cinnamon stick (just soak the buckwheat). In the morning instead of apple and orange use a similar amount of fresh pineapple and mango (you can use frozen pineapple and mango, defrosted). Make a tropical fruit sauce using the Fruit Sauce recipe (page 141) but using fresh or defrosted mango instead of the cranberries and frozen pineapple instead of the raspberries. Leave out the orange. Mix the soaked buckwheat with the cut fruit and some of the fruit sauce. (You can keep extra fruit sauce in the fridge or freezer to drink later as a smoothie.) Serve.

puffy whole-grain pancakes

I've always loved good, fluffy buttermilk pancakes. At the camp where I was the cook, I had a great homemade buttermilk pancake recipe (I would make 400 pancakes to a batch!). When I made those, lots more got eaten by the 12-year-old campers than when I made pancakes from a mix. My buttermilk pancakes were light and fluffy, but at the same time satisfying. This recipe tastes just the same, but it is whole grain and a blender pancake recipe, which means you can add the grains whole to your blender instead of using flour. The millet in the recipe keeps the color and texture light and fluffy.

INGREDIENTS	1X	2X
kefir	8 oz. (1 cup)	16 oz. (2 cups)
water	2 oz. (¼ cup)	4 oz. (½ cup)
whole Kamut or wheat berries	5½ oz. (¾ cup)	11 oz. (1½ cups)
whole millet	3½ oz. (½ cup)	7 oz. (1 cup)
coconut oil	2 Tbsp. (1 oz.)	¼ cup (2 oz.)
real maple syrup	1 Tbsp. (½ oz.)	2 Tbsp (1 oz.)
baking powder	1 tsp.	2 tsp.
baking soda	½ tsp.	1 tsp.
salt	¼ tsp.	½ tsp.
egg	1 egg	2 eggs
Makes:	12 4–5" pancakes	24 4–5" pancakes

INSTRUCTIONS

1. Place the kefir, water, and grains in your blender along with the coconut oil and maple syrup. Run blender at highest speed until mixture gets a little warm and is no longer gritty. (Since the egg hasn't been added yet, you can safely taste it to see how the texture is.) Let stand 5–10 minutes (this will allow the grains to soak up some of the liquids).

2. Meanwhile measure the baking powder, baking soda, and salt into a small bowl. Crack the egg into another small bowl. After the rest time, pour egg and the rest of the dry ingredients into the blender. Pulse 2–3 times or until just combined.

3. Cook on hot buttered griddle set to somewhere between 325 and 335 degrees.

TIPS AND VARIATIONS

- As a topping for these pancakes, I like to mix maple syrup with cream or half and half (equal parts of syrup and cream), When poured over the pancakes this sauce creates a "Tres Leches" effect.
- These pancakes store well in the freezer. I sometimes take out a frozen pancake, heat it up in the toaster, and eat it with my morning green smoothie.
- For blueberry pancakes, you can add 1 cup fresh blueberries (for the 1x recipe) after the batter is mixed. Pulse briefly once or twice—you want to chop the blueberries but not turn the batter blue.
- For sourdough pancake flavor, use all kefir instead of kefir and water.

grapefruit and blackberry fruit salad

As I started getting more into eating fresh fruits, it occurred to me one day that grapefruit and blackberries would taste good together. I gave it a try and it was delicious. I've since taken this salad to several parties—where it has quickly disappeared!

INGREDIENTS	SMALL BATCH	LARGE BATCH
fresh blackberries	6-oz. pkg.	16- to 18-oz. pkg.
refrigerated grapefruit segments	1 (20-oz.) jar	1 (64-oz.) jar

INSTRUCTIONS

1. Wash the blackberries and let them drain well.

2. Open the grapefruit slices and pour them into a serving bowl. Add the blackberries and gently stir to combine. Serve well chilled.

TIPS AND VARIATIONS

- Some of the refrigerated grapefruit slices are packaged with water and artificial sweetener—but you have to look closely at the label to notice. I don't recommend you get this kind for a couple of reasons. First, I don't trust artificial sweeteners, and second, some people have a gene that makes artificial sweeteners taste terribly bitter, so it's a good thing to stay away from, especially if you are going to serve this salad at a party.
- When washing blackberries, I use my sink sprayer with the water on high. This won't hurt good blackberries but will make ones that are too ripe fall apart. That way you can see which ones are bad and can avoid putting them in your salad.
- It's not quite as pretty, but you can use frozen mixed berries instead of fresh blackberries.

huevos rancheros

We like to eat this recipe for breakfast on the weekend when we have a little more time or for supper on a weeknight. It is a little bit more complicated than most of my recipes but is so worth it! You can make it with eggs if you feel like getting some animal protein in your diet or with avocado for a delicious vegan version. Because my Ranchero sauce is made with raw tomatoes (but tastes almost like a traditional cooked sauce), it has a higher nutrient value.

INGREDIENTS	1X	4X
Pico de Gallo (page 166)	1X batch or 8 oz.	4X batch or 32 oz.
avocado	one half	two
black beans or pinto beans	1 (16-oz.) can	4 (16-oz.) cans
dry granulated garlic (for beans)	2 tsp.	3 Tbsp.
water	1 cup	1 quart
yellow onion	½ onion (3½ oz.)	2 whole onions
V-8 juice	1 (5½ oz.) can	20–24 oz.
agave, maple syrup or sugar	1–2 tsp.	1–3 Tbsp.
chili powder	1 tsp.	4 tsp.
dry oregano—ground or leaf	½ tsp. ground or 1 tsp. leaf	2 tsp. ground or 4 tsp. leaf
dry granulated garlic (for sauce)	1 tsp.	4 tsp.
fresh tomatoes at room temperature	6 oz.	24 oz.
eggs (optional)	2–4	8–16
tortilla chips	12–16 large chips	48–64 large chips
Makes—beans:	1½ cups	6 cups
Makes—ranchero sauce:	1 cup	4 cups
Serves:	2	8

INSTRUCTIONS

1. Prepare Pico de Gallo (page 166) or use store-bought pico de gallo. Remove peel and pit from avocado (see video instructions on my website, www.MichelesGreenSmoothies.com). If doing the vegan version of this recipe, cut the avocado in quarters and then cut diagonal slices. Set aside. If doing the egg version, cut the avocado into small cubes and carefully stir the cubes into the Pico de Gallo.

2. Open, drain and rinse the beans. Pour them into a large frying pan and add the dry garlic (you can use pressed fresh garlic cloves if you prefer.) Add water and bring to a high simmer. As the beans cook, use a potato masher to crush about half the beans. If you don't have a potato masher, you can grind about half the beans in a small food processor before adding them to the pan. When the beans have thickened, transfer them to a different container and set them in the microwave to keep warm while you do the next steps.

3. Chop the onion. Add it to the frying pan where you cooked the beans along with a little oil, and sauté on medium heat until they are cooked through and starting to brown. While the onions cook, start preparing your eggs in another pan. You can poach or fry or fry over-easy—however you like them. You can do 1 or 2 eggs per serving as desired.

4. Add the V-8 juice, agave and spices (chili powder, oregano, and second garlic) to the pan with the onions. Simmer on medium high heat until the V-8 evaporates and the sauce resembles a thick paste (takes just a couple of minutes).

5. Transfer this paste to a blender and add the tomatoes. Pulse until just combined. Check on the beans. If they have cooled down too much, microwave them briefly so they are nice and hot.

6. Assemble the huevos rancheros on individual plates or shallow bowls. Put about one cup of beans in a layer on the bottom, top with a single layer of tortilla chips (about 4 per serving). Drizzle with some of the ranchero sauce. Place 1–2 eggs or several slices of avocado on top. Drizzle with more ranchero sauce and top with Pico de Gallo. Garnish with a couple more tortilla chips.

TIPS

- If you are doing the 4x batch, you will need a large, high-sided frying pan or electric fry pan, wok, or saucepan. Larger batches of beans and ranchero sauce may take longer to cook depending on the size of your pan.
- I don't usually like to use chili powder because it is a spice blend and I generally like to blend my own spices. In this recipe, though, it has the flavor profile I am looking for. You can instead use some sweet ground paprika, a dash of cayenne, and some cumin.
- If you have adobo sauce on hand, the ranchero sauce flavor is enhanced by adding half a teaspoon to the 1x batch.
- Pico tastes best made fresh but can be made up to 24 hours in advance to save time.
- Onions sauté better with a light sprinkle of salt.

blender corn muffins

I've loved corn bread as long as I can remember. I still remember the flavor of the corn bread served at Ivar's Salmon House in Seattle when I ate there at age four. Maybe I was imprinted on Ivar's recipe, but I've always loved a less sweet, slightly more dense corn bread. I love this recipe because it is moist, has the taste of fresh-ground grain, and the convenience of mixing it in a blender.

Note: This recipe is easiest to do in a high-power blender. If you have a regular blender, see "sharp-blade blender variation" below.

INGREDIENTS	
kefir	1 cup (8 oz.)
olive oil	¼ cup (4 oz.)
butter	¼ cup (4 oz.)
corn, canned or frozen	1 (8-oz.) can or 6–8 oz. frozen
agave or maple syrup	¼ cup (4 oz.)
kamut	½ cup (~3 oz.)
millet	½ cup (~3 ½ oz.)
popping corn	¾ cup (~5 ½ oz.)
baking powder	1 tsp.
baking soda	½ tsp.
salt	¾ tsp.
egg	1 egg
Makes:	24 muffins

INSTRUCTIONS

1. Place the kefir, olive oil, butter, canned or frozen corn, agave, and grains in your blender. Run blender at highest speed until the mixture gets a little warm and looks smooth. Let stand 10–20 minutes (this will allow the grains to soak up some of the liquids). Taste the batter (there's no egg in it yet, so you can.) If it seems too "gritty," you may want to run it longer.

2. Meanwhile measure the baking powder, baking soda, and salt into a small bowl. Crack the egg into another small bowl. After the rest time, pour the egg and the rest of the dry ingredients into the blender. Pulse 2–3 times or until just combined.

3. Pour into greased or lined standard muffin tins, filling each tin ¾ full.

4. Bake at 400 degrees for 15 minutes. Let rest 5–10 minutes, and then remove from pans.

TIPS AND VARIATIONS

- Sharp-blade blender variation: The sharp-blade blender I have doesn't do a great job grinding the popcorn. Soaking the corn overnight doesn't seem to help. If you have a sharp-blade blender, your best option is probably to use preground flours and measure them by weight, using the weights given in the recipe for the various grains.
- These are moistest on the day you bake them. If you have leftovers, freeze them to use another day.

super-easy no-knead bread

This bread isn't whole grain. Or super healthy. It's just really good. With a minimum of effort, it comes out tasting like a cross between French bread and sourdough and looking like a gorgeous artisan loaf. It's one of those pleasures in life that makes eating all the vegetables more fun. Maybe it's the exception to prove the rule. Whatever it is, this super-simple no-knead bread is one of my most requested recipes. And it's so easy. Maybe sometime I'll come up with a whole grain version that's just as good and just as easy. In the meantime, I love cutting a loaf of this open, spreading it with good butter, and just enjoying it . . .

Note: This recipe requires having an ovenproof pot with a tight-fitting lid. I use a cast-iron Dutch oven. It does have to rise for about 8 hours. It takes very little work, but it does take a little planning.

INGREDIENTS	SMALL LOAF	LARGE LOAF
white bread flour	3 cups (1 lb.)	6 cups (2 lbs.)
instant dry yeast	½ tsp.	1 tsp.
salt	1½ tsp.	3 tsp.
filtered water	1½ cups (12 oz.)	3 cups (24 oz.)

INSTRUCTIONS

1. Mix the dry ingredients together with a spoon in a bowl. Add water and stir until combined—it doesn't have to look perfectly mixed. Cover with a lid. Let stand covered at room temperature for about 8 hours.

2. Preheat your oven to 450 degrees. Place your baking pot in the oven to preheat with the oven (it needs to be hot when you put the dough in).

3. When oven and pot are hot, take out the pot and pour the dough in, using a spatula to scrape the dough out of the bowl. It doesn't matter what the dough looks like at this point, as long as it is in a single lump. Put the hot lid on the pot quickly and return it to the oven.

4. Bake at 425 degrees for about 20–25 minutes. Crust should be light brown.

5. Remove lid and bake for about 10 minutes or until the crust is as firm, brown, or crispy as you would like it to be.

6. Remove bread from the baking pot (it should slide out easily). Cool for at least one hour before cutting. If the bread seems slightly too moist, it will be a better consistency the next day.

TIPS AND VARIATIONS

- If you haven't heard of no-knead bread, you should look it up online. In my recipe I eliminate a couple of the original steps and make what was already an elegantly simple way to produce rustic bread even more simple. For more detail, visit my website: www.MichelesGreenSmoothies.com

- The small loaf batch will fit in a 10-inch pot. The large loaf batch fits best in a 12-inch or larger pot.
- This recipe must be made with bread flour or with gluten-enhanced flour. You can substitute whole wheat bread flour, but will need an extra 3–4 tablespoons water per batch, and the bread will be heavier.
- If you aren't able to bake the dough after 8 hours, put it in the fridge and bake it the next day.
- If your bread sticks, next time try spraying the pot with cooking spray or dusting it with flour just before adding the dough. My favorite butter to have on bread is European cultured butter. It used to be hard to find in the United States but is now much more available. As it turns out, butter in the States is generally made by mechanical means (churning) while butter in Europe is made by culturing the cream. I particularly like the European-style cultured pasture butter from Organic Valley that is made from the milk of cows that have fed in green summer meadows. I think it tastes better and there is evidence that butter made from the milk of cows fed on greens has beneficial compounds that aren't found in other butters.
- I usually leave the bread out for three to four hours after baking. After that, if there is any bread left, I slice it and keep it in a plastic bag on the counter. The crust will retain its chewy texture but will soften slightly.
- Herb Variation: For the small loaf batch stir in the following with the dry ingredients: 2 tablespoons dill weed and 1 tablespoon dry granulated onion.

SECTION 5

Appetizers, Dips, and Dressings

- A LITTLE FAT IS A GOOD THING
- RECIPES
- FREQUENTLY ASKED QUESTIONS

A LITTLE FAT IS A GOOD THING

In the far north of Germany, there used to be something called "Butter Cruises"—*Butterfahrten*. They started because the northern Germans loved Danish butter. If they took a cruise to one of the nearby Danish islands, they could get Danish butter and also buy duty-free goods! Eventually the butter cruises became about much more than butter and duty-free items. They became a way for retired northern Germans to get out on the sea (which they love) and spend an afternoon doing something different. The butter-ferry lines, seeing that their clientele were mostly senior citizens, provided entertainment, food, and tables to play bridge. Clubs were formed and the ferry rides were affordable enough that some folks went on a *Butterfarht* as often as five days a week!

What's the point to this story? Not much, except that it shows how much Germans value high-quality dairy. The French, Swiss, Scandinavians, and Austrians do too. There is nowhere in the world where you can buy more varieties of high-quality yogurt than in Germany. In France and Switzerland cheese connoisseurs say they can tell from the taste of a cheese where it came from because of the flavor of the herbs and flowers the cows were eating. In small towns in Austria, people can still walk to the local dairy, leave their coins and scoop up their own fresh milk.

In America, our food industries developed differently, and in some cases, quantity became more important than quality. As I try to Eat Green, I am always trying to maximize the nutrients I get from my food. While dairy—as has been too well advertised—contains calcium, leafy greens are actually a much better source of that critical mineral. In every possible way, greens exceed dairy as a provider of vitamins and minerals. So what role does dairy have in a green diet? There is one important thing that dairy can provide, and that is fat. What? Fat? Yes, fat. Fat can be a good thing. And in the case of high-quality dairy, it can also be a truly delicious experience.

My dad and older brother are research physiologists. As I was growing up, dinner table conversations often revolved around nerve function. Terms like "lipid-bilayer"(which

refers to the structure of a cell wall) and "myelin sheath" (an electrical insulator essential to nervous system function) were subjects frequently discussed. Both of these critical body components contain fat. That's not to say that we need tons of fat; most of us in the United States get lots more than we need. But we are so used to thinking of fat in the body as something bad, that we are trying to get rid of, that I think it helps to step back for a moment and see that fats fulfill some vital physiological functions.

A 2004 study on salad dressings explained another critical function of fat in the body. In the study, test subjects were asked to eat three different salads on three different days. The salads would be served with a certain portion of dressing. One salad would have fat-free dressing, one would have low-fat dressing, and one would have a normal "fat" dressing. After eating each salad, blood tests would be performed to show whether any of the micronutrients in the salad would show up in the blood stream. The title of the paper sums up the results of the tests very nicely: "Carotenoid bioavailability is higher from salads ingested with full-fat than with fat-reduced salad dressings as measured with electrochemical detection." In other words, the body absorbs some nutrients better in the presence of fat. (Research published in the *American Journal of Clinical Nutrition*. Abstract can be found here: http://ajcn.nutrition.org/content/80/2/396.abstract.)

Throughout my lifetime the research has gone back and forth on which fats are "good" and which are "bad." Me, I think I will stick with trying to limit the amount of fats I consume in general and try to make the ones I do eat high quality and flavorful . . . ones that will help me Eat Green.

the veggie tray

A section on vegetable appetizers wouldn't be complete without mentioning the veggie tray. People older than I am have occasionally commented, "Veggies used to be called vegetables!" I'm not sure just when it happened—probably sometime in the '80s—but the language changed around the time when veggie trays became popular. On this page, I'm going to try to give you a few ideas that you may not already have had for ways to eat veggies fresh and as a finger food.

MY TOP FIVE FAVORITE UNUSUAL VEGGIES FOR A VEGGIE TRAY:

1. Jicama—it's just so crisp and delicious! (See page 77.)
2. Artichoke hearts—okay, it's not a raw veggie, but they are really good! (See page 76.)
3. Baby green onions, trimmed—they look pretty and are a fun break from the other veggies.
4. Sugar snap peas—they add color and make a veggie tray seem special. (See page 36.)
5. Fresh sliced cucumbers—they aren't on trays you can buy because they don't keep. They have to be added at the last minute and that makes them at least a little bit special. Sliced cucumbers taste amazing with Elaine's Ranch Dressing, page 176.

SOME OTHER FUN VEGETABLE SNACKS:

- Chilled radishes with salt. If you haven't tried this, you should. The salt mellows the sharp radish flavor and kids and adults enjoy dipping radishes in a bowl of sea salt. To prepare the radishes, wash, trim the ends, and soak in ice water. If you want make them prettier (and make the salt stick better), make a few cuts in the radishes so that when you put them in the ice water they will turn into "flowers." Make sure to drain and dry the radishes before putting them out for dipping.
- Whole real carrots—we have gotten so used to the convenience of baby carrots, that we sometimes forget there is such a thing as a whole carrot. Whole carrots tend to be a little sweeter than baby carrots. It can be a pain to cut them into carrot sticks, but you can also eat them whole. Just scrub or peel and bite. It's kind of fun. Makes you feel like saying, "Uhhh, what's up, doc?"
- Raw broccoli florets with olive oil and salt. See page 132.
- Soaked raw chickpeas with olive oil, salt, and garlic. See page 164.

For more veggie tray ideas, look at my list of unusual vegetables, starting on page 76, or go online and look up *crudites* for French versions of the veggie tray.

stuffed mushrooms

My husband loves stuffed mushrooms, so we have tried out quite a few different kinds over the years. This recipe that I invented for a party a few years ago is our favorite.

INGREDIENTS	1X	2X
baby Bella or button mushrooms	2 (8-oz.) packs or 1 lb.	2 lb.
butter	3–4 Tbsp.	6–8 Tbsp.
minced garlic (fridge)	1–2 tsp.	1 Tbsp.
dry granulated onion	2 tsp.	1½ Tbsp.
Ritz-style whole-grain crackers	2 oz. (about 20 crackers)	4 oz. (about 40 crackers)
shredded Parmesan	3–4 Tbsp.	about ½ cup
broth	1–4 Tbsp.	2–8 Tbsp.
Makes:	about 32 stuffed mushrooms	about 64 stuffed mushrooms

INSTRUCTIONS

1. Remove stems from mushrooms and finely dice. Melt the butter in a sauté pan and add the garlic and mushroom stems. Sauté the mushroom stems over medium-high heat for about 10 minutes. If the butter starts to brown too much, turn down the heat.

2. Break up the crackers into fine crumbs. Pour the cracker crumbs into the pan along with the granulated onion. Remove the pan from the heat. Stir in the Parmesan.

3. Add just enough broth to give the mixture a stuffing-like consistency.

4. Fill the mushroom caps with the filling, slightly mounding the filling in each mushroom. You will need an average of 1–1½ teaspoons filling per mushroom, depending on size.

5. Place the mushrooms on a lined baking sheet. Bake at 375 degrees for about 35 minutes or until the stuffing is lightly brown on top. Let stand 5–10 minutes before serving.

TIPS AND VARIATIONS

- Some people say never to wash mushrooms with water, to just rub off any dirt. I personally do wash my mushrooms by running each one under warm water and gently rubbing, and then allowing them to drain in a colander or on a paper towel. This has always worked fine for me. Do whatever works best for you.
- I generally use whole-grain Ritz for this recipe and make my cracker crumbs by putting the crackers in a bag and squishing them with my fingers until they are the size of bread crumbs. If you prefer, you can use dry bread crumbs or dry gluten-free bread crumbs. If you use bread crumbs you may need to add some salt since the crackers I use are salted. I use crackers rather than dry bread crumbs because they don't go stale as quickly and are more versatile.
- You can use whatever kind of broth you want for this recipe. I generally use the refrigerated paste broth concentrate for this recipe and make it up a little bit strong—it gives the stuffing more flavor. How much broth you need will depend on how much water evaporates as you cook your diced mushroom stems.
- These stuffed mushrooms reheat well. They can be refrigerated for a few days or frozen longer and then reheated in the microwave or in the oven.

horseradish gazpacho

Every Christmas Eve, my in-laws served a tomato-horseradish-shrimp drink that I absolutely loved. This recipe is a cross between that and gazpacho—the cold tomato soup from Spain.

INGREDIENTS	1X	2X
fresh or frozen tomatoes	12 oz.	24 oz.
red onion	½ oz.	1 oz.
dry granulated onion	½ Tbsp.	1 Tbsp.
lemon juice	¼ cup	½ cup
salt	¼ tsp.	½ tsp.
olive oil	1 tsp.	2 tsp.
agave or sugar	1 tsp.	2 tsp.
prepared horseradish	2–4 tsp.	1–3 Tbsp.
finely grated celery root	½ oz.	1 oz.
finely sliced leek	⅓ oz.	⅔ oz.
avocado	¼ to ½	½ to 1 whole
Makes (without avocado):	2 cups	4 cups
Serves (with avocado):	2 to 3	4 to 6

INSTRUCTIONS

1. Wash and quarter the tomatoes (or use frozen quartered tomatoes).

2. Place tomatoes in a blender or food processor. Add the fresh onion, dry onion, lemon juice, salt, olive oil, agave or sugar, and horseradish. Pulse until mixed. Tomatoes should be slightly chunky.

3. Sir in the finely sliced leeks and grated celery root. Refrigerate 30 minutes to 24 hours before serving.

4. Peel the avocado and cut it into small cubes. Gently stir it into the soup.

5. Serve like a soup with a spoon.

TIPS AND VARIATIONS

- This recipe is a great way to use up fresh tomatoes if you have a garden. When I have access to extra garden tomatoes, I often cut them in quarters and freeze them. My frozen tomatoes (defrosted) also work great in this recipe. Using fresh or frozen tomatoes rather than canned or bottled increases the nutrient value of this recipe.
- If you like things zippy, you can add more horseradish, a splash of Worcestershire, or a drop or two of hot sauce.
- You can serve this as described in the recipe with cubed avocado or substitute salad shrimp. Or use both.

easy chickpea snack

Dry chickpeas, also called garbanzo beans, are easy to keep on hand and are high in fiber, protein, iron, and vitamin B-6. When soaked, they taste a little like fresh garden peas and have a satisfying crunch. Recipes for roasted chickpeas have become very popular, but I think they taste even better soaked and prepared without roasting. I happened onto this fact one day when I was preparing some for roasting, and my niece and her little boy were here. All three of us couldn't stop munching on the soaked garbanzo beans as prepared in this recipe!

INGREDIENTS	1X	2X
dry garbanzo beans a.k.a chickpeas	8 ounces	1 (1-lb.) bags
hot water for soaking	3 cups	6 cups
olive oil	½ tsp.	1 tsp.
salt	⅛ tsp.	¼ tsp.
dry granulated garlic (optional)	¼ tsp.	½ tsp.
Makes:	~2 cups	~4 cups

INSTRUCTIONS

1. Measure out desired amount of dry garbanzo beans. Immerse the beans in hot water. You will need twice as much water as the volume of beans used.

2. Allow to soak overnight or for 8–12 hours.

3. When the beans have a nice crunch but aren't chewy at all, drain the water, rinse them, and spread them out on paper towels to dry.

4. Transfer them to a bowl and add the olive oil, salt, and garlic powder. Stir until the chickpeas are coated. Enjoy! If you don't eat them all raw/soaked, roast the rest.

TIPS AND VARIATIONS

- Roasted Variation: Prepare the chickpeas as above. Spread them out in a single layer on a lined baking sheet, keeping them toward the middle. Bake at 400 degrees for 30 minutes, shaking the tray or using a spatula to turn the chickpeas every ten minutes. The chickpeas are done when the smallest ones are getting too brown. If the smallest ones aren't slightly overdone, the large ones will have a mushy texture. Store in a bag or container.
- If your beans are old, you may need to soak them for longer. For more information on soaking, see pages 108 and 170.

pika's pico de gallo

At the camp I worked at for many years, my camp name was "Pika." One of my most popular recipes was my salsa. It was actually just bottled salsa mixed half and half with fresh diced tomatoes, but it tasted really good and had more nutrients than just plain bottled salsa. I still make that when I'm in a hurry, but pico de gallo made from scratch tastes even better, has more vitamins, and is easier to make than you would think—you just need a really good tomato cutting knife.

INGREDIENTS	1X	4X
fresh lime juice	~2 tsp. (about ½ lime, juiced)	~4 tsp.
cayenne pepper	a dash	⅛ tsp
dry granulated garlic	½–1 tsp.	1–2 tsp.
salt	¼ tsp.	½ tsp.
green onions or red onion	3–4 green onions or 1½ oz. red onion	6–8 green onions or 3 oz. red onion
diced fresh tomatoes	1 cup or 6–7 oz.	2 cups or 12–14 oz.
cilantro (leaves only)	about 20 stems or ¼ oz.	about ½ oz.
Makes:	about 1 cup	about 2 cups
Serves:	2	8

INSTRUCTIONS

1. In a bowl, combine the lime juice, cayenne pepper, granulated garlic, and salt.

2. Finely snip your green onions or dice your red onion, and stir into the other ingredients.

3. Carefully dice the fresh tomatoes. Wash and finely snip the leaves of your cilantro. Stir these carefully together with the other ingredients. Let stand about a half hour to allow the flavors to blend.

4. Serve alongside my Guacamole (page 168).

pika's guacamole

With guacamole, less is more (assuming you have good avocados!). I have had a lot of people ask me how I make my guacamole, and it's the simplicity of this recipe that makes it delicious.

INGREDIENTS	1X	2X
ripe Haas avocado	1	2
dry granulated onion	heaping ¼ tsp.	½–¾ tsp.
salt	⅛ tsp.	¼ tsp.
fresh lime juice	1–2 Tbsp. (juice of half a lime)	3–4 Tbsp. (juice of one lime)
Greek yogurt or sour cream (optional)	1–2 Tbsp.	2–4 Tbsp.
Serves:	1 to 2	2 to 3

INSTRUCTIONS

1. Cut the avocados in half, remove the pit, and scoop the avocado out into a bowl with a flat bottom.

2. Sprinkle the onion and salt over the avocado. Add the fresh-squeezed lime juice (no substitutions!) and Greek yogurt or sour cream if desired.

3. Mash the avocado and mix the ingredients together as you mash. For small batches, I use a fork and for large batches a potato masher. Serve with tortilla chips and salsa or my Pico de Gallo.

TIPS

- Part of what makes this guacamole so yummy is the texture. Don't make it in a food processor. It will get too smooth and it won't be as good.
- Choose ripe avocados for this recipe that you can easily smash with a fork.
- The lime juice and sour cream/Greek yogurt keep the guacamole from going brown right away. You can even refrigerate it and have it be just about as good the next day. To refrigerate, cover the guacamole with plastic wrap so that the wrap is right against the surface of the guacamole. If some parts of the surface have turned brown the next day, just stir it up. The overall color and flavor will not be affected.

the best hummus

I've been experimenting with hummus for a long time. I have liked making hummus from canned garbanzo beans because it was so easy (and tasted better than any store-bought hummus I could find), but I didn't love the fact that some or even most canned garbanzos had a strange aftertaste. I had also tried making hummus from dry beans, soaked and cooked, but didn't like the extra step of cooking the beans. This recipe, which uses dry beans simply soaked, is just as easy as my canned bean recipe, has a higher nutrient value, and has a delicious "fluffy" texture.

INGREDIENTS	1X	2X
dry garbanzo beans	4 oz. (¼ of a 16-oz. bag)	8 oz. (half of a 16-oz. bag)
hot water for soaking	1½ cups	3 cups
olive oil	3 Tbsp.	6 Tbsp.
water	2–2½ Tbsp.	4–5 Tbsp.
fresh squeezed lemon juice	1 ½ –2 Tbsp.	3–4 Tbsp.
dry granulated garlic	2 tsp.	4 tsp.
minced garlic (fridge)(optional)	1 tsp. or 1 clove	2 tsp. or 2 cloves
toasted sesame oil	½ tsp.	1 tsp.
salt	½ tsp.	1 tsp.
cumin	¼–½ tsp.	½–1 tsp.
Makes:	about 1½ cups	about 3 cups

INSTRUCTIONS

1. Place the garbanzo beans in a container and add the hot water. Allow to soak overnight or for at least 10 hours. The chickpeas at this point should be crunchy but not too chewy.

2. Thoroughly drain the garbanzo beans, rinse them and place them in a food processor. Process until finely chopped, then add the other ingredients. If you like a milder hummus, leave out the fresh garlic.

3. Process until a smooth dip forms. Refrigerate until ready to serve. For best flavor, refrigerate for 24 hours before serving. Serve with fresh veggies, rice crackers, or other crackers.

TIPS AND VARIATIONS

- About Soaking: Soaking seeds starts the sprouting process and activates beneficial nutrients that are dormant in the seed, making them more nutritious than a seed that is simply cooked. Soaked or sprouted beans also seem to have fewer digestive side effects because the proteins in the bean are altered during the sprouting process. For more information on soaking garbanzo beans, see pages 108 and 164.
- Traditional hummus recipes often call for sesame tahini. I don't like having to keep this ingredient on hand since I would only use it for hummus and I also don't love the bitter flavor it often brings. Instead, I use toasted sesame oil, usually used for Asian cooking. It has a similar flavor profile to tahini, is easier to keep on hand, and more versatile (since I also use it in Asian cooking), and it is less bitter. If you don't have it, you can use regular sesame oil instead of the olive oil or simply leave it out.
- Other ingredients: In this recipe it is critical to have fresh lemon juice and fresh, high-quality olive oil. If your olive oil has a harsh flavor at all, it will come through in the dip.

Salad Dressings 101

DRESSING BASICS

As I have talked to people about this book, I find that a lot of people are intimidated by salad dressing recipes. Actually, I was too. I used to look at dressing recipes with seven to ten ingredients and wonder if it would be worth the effort. When I started eating green, I started experimenting with simple dressings and learned some basic concepts about salad dressings. Now I can look at a recipe, analyze why each ingredient is there, and make a guess about what it will taste like. Here are some of the things I've learned:

1. Almost every dressing has an acid ingredient like lemon juice or vinegar.

2. Most dressings have an oil of some kind. This can be something like olive oil or mayonnaise or it could be a dairy product like sour cream. Or a combination. Some blender recipes call for seeds as a substitute for some of the oil.

3. Many recipes have some kind of sweetener to mellow the sharpness of the acid. The sweetener in a recipe can be sugar, agave, or honey; it can also be fruit—fresh or dried—or fruit juices such as apple juice and pineapple juice.

4. Because, as they say, "water and oil don't mix," some dressings have an emulsifier—something to keep the oily ingredients from separating from the watery ones. Traditional emulsifiers include egg and mustard. Dairy in a dressing works as an emulsifier (as well as being like an oil) and ground seeds can also fulfill that function. Adding mayo to any dressing can emulsify it.

5. Flavorful ingredients in the salad can be paired with a simple dressing to result in a more complex flavor overall. As an example, in My Arugula Salad, the dressing is simple but the red onion flavors the salad as a whole.

6. Some dressings add salt, spices, and other ingredients for flavor. Mustard adds flavor as well as acting as an emulsifier. Soy sauce, Worcestershire sauce, garlic, onion, ginger, and dry herbs can also be used to bring more flavor to a dressing. The ingredients you use to flavor your dressing define the flavor profile. You can use the following information on flavor profiles to create your own dressings:

- Asian: Critical flavors are garlic and ginger. Sesame seeds and soy sauce are frequently added. Green onions can be used anywhere while fresh cilantro evokes more of a Thai or Vietnamese theme. For a teriyaki flavor, use pineapple juice with soy sauce and garlic. For heat, use red pepper flakes or Mongolian fire oil. Use sesame oil for the oil and rice vinegar for the acid.
- Mexican: Critical flavors are cumin, garlic, and onion. For more of an enchilada flavor, use ground oregano with the cumin.
- Greek: Critical flavors are oregano, onion, and garlic. Also basil, marjoram, and mint. Red wine vinegar, balsamic vinegar, and olive oil go well and also yogurt. Cucumber can be used as an ingredient and emulsifier in Greek dressings.
- Italian: Critical flavors are basil and garlic. Also pine nuts, onion, and rosemary. Olive oil is the oil of choice.
- Middle Eastern: Critical flavors are ground coriander seed and cumin. Onion and garlic are also important along with fresh herbs like parsley and cilantro. Sesame seeds and sesame oil enhance the flavors.

DRESSINGS TO BUY

While I don't mind making my own dressings now, I like the convenience of store-bought ones. I tend to be pretty choosy about them though. I try to choose dressings with relatively short ingredient lists, but mostly I try to choose dressings that will be really flavorful. This is my current list of store-bought dressings I love. (This list includes dressings I have already mentioned in recipes.)

- *Creamy Garlic Salad Dressing from Follow Your Heart.* This dressing is so delicious, I bring it to any party I go to now where I am bringing a tossed salad. It is dairy free, gluten free, and vegan, but you would never guess it from the taste. The same brand makes a really excellent Thousand Island and a classic Ranch.
- *Spicy Peanut Vinaigrette from Trader Joe's.* I have tried several bottled Asian dressings and have yet to find anything that comes even close to this Trader Joe's dressing in terms of flavor. It's worth going out of your way for.
- *"Little Green Packet" Salad dressings.* Anyone who has spent time anywhere in Europe is probably familiar with these convenient dry dressing mixes from Knorr. You can buy them at specialty stores in the US or online. If you are looking for them online, look up "Knorr Salat Kroenung." It comes in flavors like "Dill and Herbs" or "Garden Herbs." To make these dressings, measure 3 tablespoons water, 3 tablespoons oil, add the packet, and whisk or shake. I will often take a small container of oil on a trip with me and one of these packets. Then I buy bags of prewashed lettuce and just mix up the dressing when I want to. The flavor of these dressings is very similar to the flavor profile of the dressing recipe for Colorful Vegetable Salad.
- *Olive Garden Dressing.* It was a happy day for salad lovers when Olive Garden started selling their dressing in stores. When I'm going to a get-together where I'm not sure whether people like salad or not, I usually bring my Caesar salad or else my version of an Olive Garden salad with Olive Garden Dressing on the side.
- *Lighthouse Caesar-Caesar.* Lighthouse has a few different kinds of refrigerated Caesar dressings. This one is my favorite (see page 39).

DRESSING RECIPES IN THIS BOOK

There are a few dressing recipes in this section, but most of my dressing recipes are in the salad section. Here is a list of dressing recipes in this book:

- *Walt's Coleslaw dressing.* It's just a blend of premade dressings, but it's convenient and a good combination. Page 41.
- *Simple Creamy Greek Dressing.* In the Tips on page 48. Only takes a few ingredients.
- *Simple Marinade.* With Betty's Marinated Cucumbers, page 46. Works well with sliced sweet onions.
- *Colorful Vegetable Salad.* This is a light dill vinaigrette. Page 50.
- *Arugula Salad Dressing.* This sweet three-ingredient dressing works well on green salads that have nuts and dried or fresh fruit. Page 52.
- *Classic French Vinaigrette.* This is just what it says—a versatile vinaigrette from the country that probably invented the vinaigrette. Page 55.
- *Root's Café Lemon Basil Dressing.* A four-ingredient creamy dressing that can go on any tossed salad. Page 67.
- *Asian Dressing and Marinade.* The dressing I made up to go on my Seared Ahi Salad. Page 73.
- *Easy Chia Mayo.* This mayo uses chia as an emulsifier instead of egg.
- *Elaine's Ranch Dressing.* The best ranch dressing I have ever eaten.
- *Michele's Lime-Cilantro Dressing.* A good dressing for any southwestern style salad or wrap.
- *Easy Homemade Caesar.* Something you can use instead of the Lighthouse Caesar.

easy chia mayo

Mayo sometimes has a bad reputation. I think there are several reasons for that:

- people think it is high in fat
- people think it is associated with food poisoning cases
- it contains eggs, which tend to be controversial

Since I use mayo in several of my recipes, I'd like to address some of these common concerns.

First, mayonnaise is basically just a light vinaigrette. In fact, it may have been the first vinaigrette that could be considered "light" since it is nearly half water. Mayo is made of water, oil, vinegar or lemon juice, egg, and salt. Vegetable oils have been a traditional accompaniment of green salads for thousands of years—and now we know why. Some of the vitamins in salads are better absorbed by the body in the presence of oil, so a little oil on a salad is a good thing.

Second, when a potato salad or pasta salad goes bad, the real culprit is the potato or pasta. Bacteria love moist cooked starches, especially when they are nice and warm—and that is where the problem usually starts—with starches that aren't cooled quickly enough after cooking or are allowed to become warm. Because mayo contains either lemon juice or vinegar or both, it is higher in acid and is less likely to go bad.

Eggs are one of those foods that have been alternately praised and vilified. In mayo, egg is the emulsifier (see page 172). Since I am generally trying to increase the plant products in my diet, my mayo recipe uses chia as the emulsifier instead of egg. Using chia instead of egg changes the consistency and flavor a little. Those changes aren't very noticeable when my mayo is spread on bread or tossed in with a salad, but if you are just starting on a green diet, I would suggest using regular commercial mayo in my recipes at first since that is easier and more familiar.

INGREDIENTS	1X	3X
water	⅔ cup	2 cups
cider vinegar	1–1½ tsp	3–4½ tsp.
Dijon mustard	½ tsp.	1½ tsp.
salt	½ tsp.	1½ tsp.
white chia or ground chia	3½–4 Tbsp.	¾ cup or just less than ¾ cup
oil—see note	¾ cup	2¼ cups
Makes:	about 1½ cups	about 4½ cups

INSTRUCTIONS

1. Place all ingredients in the blender. Run blender on highest speed until the mixture is white and thick—about 45–60 seconds (any type of blender). If the blender stalls, pause to release air bubbles.

2. Transfer to a covered container and refrigerate. Mayo will become thicker when it is cold.

TIPS

- Despite the fact that it is such a small part of the dressing, the amount of vinegar you use in this recipe makes a huge difference in the flavor profile. A little less vinegar, and it tastes more like Best Foods Mayonnaise. A tiny bit more, and it goes more in the direction of Miracle Whip. Experiment and see what you like best.
- Research on oils goes back and forth on what oils are most and least healthy. In this recipe I like using an oil that has a light neutral flavor. Some oils with neutral flavors include "extra light" olive oil, grape seed oil, and the ubiquitous Canola oil. You can use coconut oil for up to a quarter of the oil in the recipe, but if you use more than that the flavor profile and the consistency will be quite different.
- The slight chia seed flavor will get a little bit stronger with time. This mayo will keep a maximum of two weeks, but I recommend using it within the first few days. (This doesn't matter as much if you are using it as a base for another dressing with stronger flavors.)

elaine's ranch dressing

This dressing is based on an amazing dressing made by Chiz's Restaurant in St. Anthony, Idaho. They sell their dressing in supermarkets near the restaurant, but since I don't live there, I love having the chance to make my own. Elaine's version is based on hints she received from friends of friends who had worked there. I think her version actually tastes better than the original—something I didn't think was possible!

INGREDIENTS	1X	2X
Best Foods mayo	1 cup	2 cups
buttermilk	½ cup	1 cup
sour cream	¼ cup	½ cup
fresh minced onion	½ tsp.	1 tsp.
dry parsley	½ Tbsp.	1 Tbsp.
black pepper	⅛ tsp.	¼ tsp.
dry dill weed	⅛ tsp.	¼ tsp.
dry basil	¼ tsp.	½ tsp.
dry granulated garlic	½ tsp.	1 tsp.
dry granulated onion	½ tsp.	1 tsp.
salt	¼ tsp.	½ tsp.
Makes:	1¾ cup	3½ cups

INSTRUCTIONS

1. Measure the mayo, buttermilk, and sour cream.

2. Cut off a small piece of onion and mince it using a garlic press. Measure out the amount of onion you need. This is an extra step, but the dressing is not the same without it.

3. Add all the other ingredients and mix. Chill at least 24 hours before using.

TIPS AND VARIATIONS

- Keep in mind the flavors from the herbs will intensify with time. While the dressing will seem perfect and mild the first several days, it may start to taste too dilly after a week.
- To make this as a dip, make the following changes in the 1x recipe: use ¾ cup mayo, ¼ cup buttermilk, and ¾ cup sour cream.
- Since this recipe aims to be the same as the one they make at the restaurant, I have left it just as it is. If you prefer, you can use kefir instead of buttermilk , Greek yogurt instead of sour cream, and my chia mayo. If using kefir and Greek yogurt you may need to add a little agave to counteract the extra sourness.

michele's lime-cilantro dressing

I created this dressing recipe in 2000 because I wanted a really good dressing to on a southwestern salad. I wanted it to have easy-to-find ingredients but have a similar flavor profile to the dressing at Café Rio restaurants. This one is all from scratch but easy to make. It is my all-time favorite southwest dressing.

INGREDIENTS	1X	4X
sour cream/Greek yogurt	1¾ cup	7 cups
mayo or chia mayo	¾ cup	3 cups
water	⅓–½ cup	1⅓–2 cups
fresh lime juice	¼ cup	1 cup
green onion (optional)	1 onion	4 onions
fresh whole cilantro, loosely packed	1½ cups	6 cups
dry granulated garlic	½–1 tsp	2–4 tsp.
salt	1½ tsp.	2 Tbsp.
cayenne pepper	¼ tsp.	1 tsp.
sugar or agave syrup	2 Tbsp.	½ cup
Makes:	~3½ cups	14 cups

INSTRUCTIONS

1. Wash the green onion and cut in pieces (if using). Place all the ingredients in a blender and purée until smooth. Chill.
2. Use on sandwiches, salads, or wraps.

TIPS

- If you need to make a bigger batch than will fit in your blender (like the 4x batch here), purée all the ingredients except the sour cream/Greek yogurt and mayo in the blender, and then whisk the blender part with the sour cream/Greek yogurt and mayo in a mixing bowl.
- Keeps about a week in the refrigerator.

easy homemade caesar

I've made this homemade version purposely a little stronger than my favorite store-bought Caesar so that you don't have to use quite as much dressing. For a milder dressing, use the low end of the ingredient amounts.

INGREDIENTS	1X	2X
minced garlic (fridge)	1 tsp.	2 tsp.
fresh lemon juice	1–1½ tsp.	2–3 tsp.
Worcestershire sauce	1–1½ tsp.	2–3 tsp.
dry granulated onion	1½ tsp.	3 tsp.
dry granulated garlic	½–1 tsp.	1–2 tsp.
Dijon or spicy brown mustard	1 tsp.	2 tsp.
fresh ground black pepper	¼ tsp.	½ tsp.
Parmesan cheese	2 Tbsp.	¼ cup
mayo or chia mayo	½ cup	1 cup
Makes:	~4 oz. (½ cup)	~8 oz. (1 cup)

INSTRUCTIONS

1. Mix all the ingredients.
2. Chill for at least 24 hours before serving. When using with my Caesar Salad recipe (page 39), leave out the splash of vinegar.

FREQUENTLY ASKED QUESTIONS

I MADE AN OLIVE OIL DRESSING AND PUT IT IN THE FRIDGE AND THE OIL WENT HARD. WHAT DO I DO?

Olive oil is solid at refrigerator temperature. To melt it, take your dressing out of the fridge and let it sit at room temperature for five to ten minutes, shake it, let it sit a little longer, and then it will be liquid again. All oils have a temperature at which they become solid. Where I live, coconut oil is liquid during the summer and solid during the winter. It becomes solid around 74 degrees.

YOU MENTION THAT YOU LIKE TO USE DAIRY PRODUCTS IN WAYS THAT WILL MAKE THE MOST DIFFERENCE IN FLAVOR OR BE THE MOST USEFUL IN EATING GREEN. WHAT ARE SOME OF THESE?

Here are some of the types of dairy I like to use and why:

- **Kefir:** Good bacteria ("probiotics") have been shown to be important to digestive function and kefir is full of good bacteria and also has some beneficial yeast. Studies seem to indicate that kefir is more beneficial than yogurt. Another way to get probiotics is to put probiotic "shots" in your smoothies. These are available in most grocery stores from the "GoodBelly" brand.
- **Salad dressings with dairy:** I think anything that helps you eat more greens is good, especially if you are just starting out Eating Green.
- **Goat cheese and sheep cheese:** these can take a little getting used to, but can be very delicious in the right context! I use them because they tend to be easier to digest and higher in nutrients than cheese from cow's milk. My favorite goat cheese is a soft cheese called *chevre* that can be purchased in logs or crumbles. In Europe, most feta is made from sheep's milk and I love the flavor. It is just starting to be available near where I live in the United States. *Chevre* or feta crumbles can add a wonderful dimension to salads. *Tip:* if you open a block of feta in liquid and the cheese seems unbearably salty, try rinsing it in cold water or letting it sit in a container of cold water for a few hours in the fridge.
- **Parmesan and other hard cheeses:** Hard cheeses like parmesan are easy to digest and contain little or no lactose. Parmesan is also high in *umami*, which simply means it has compounds that boost the "savory" flavor of the foods eaten with it. It gives you more "bang for your buck" than most other cheeses when it comes to flavor.
- **Roquefort and other "flavorful" cheeses:** As I mention in the Tips on page 55, I didn't think I was a fan of blue cheese, except in small amounts in dressing. It turns out that I still have a lot to learn about blue cheese.
- **Butter:** I don't think there is any truly definitive research on butter. I use butter because of the flavor it brings that can make it easier to eat vegetables. When possible I purchase butter from grass-fed cows since the greens the cows eat can make the butter more nutritious. (See also page 153.)
- **Whipping cream, sour cream, and Greek yogurt:** I use these sparingly in a dressing or as a topping—again to make it easier to eat fruits and vegetables. I buy the full-fat versions because they tend to be more "whole"—i.e. they have been treated and manipulated less. And if I'm only going to eat a little dairy, I would like it to be high quality.

YOU MENTION EATING HIGH-QUALITY DAIRY (AND DAIRY WHICH CONTAINS FAT). BUT ISN'T LOW-FAT DAIRY BETTER? AND AREN'T THERE HEALTHIER WAYS TO GET FATS IN A SALAD?

The nutrition research industry has been trying to answer these questions for decades. Before I tell you my thoughts on this, it can be helpful to keep in mind that when it comes to scientific studies, what the research team finds depends, to a certain extent, on what they are looking for. For example, if the dairy industry hires a team of researchers to find things about dairy that are potentially healthy, the researchers will find things about dairy that are potentially healthy; the only question is, compared to what? Years ago, studies found that people in the Mediterranean had less risk for certain diseases. The researchers tried to pin down the things that were different about the Mediterranean diet compared to ours. One of the things they found was that olive oil was the fat of choice in those areas. Out of context, we Americans started busily substituting olive oil everywhere we could. I'm not saying that was a bad thing. It was probably a good thing, but the point perhaps wasn't so much what oil they use as what else the people in the Mediterranean were eating. Based on my travel experience, in the Mediterranean people still eat a lot of vegetables. A hundred years ago, Italian immigrants to the United States were criticized by nutrition "experts" for eating too many vegetables. In our cultural context in the US, we have generally not loved or cared about vegetables, the way they do in the Mediterranean. Isn't it possible that the difference in heart disease lies in the amount of vegetables they eat, not just in the type of oil?

To the question, "aren't there healthier ways to get fats into a salad?" the answer is yes, there are healthier ways than using dairy . . . or oil. The healthiest way to get fat into a salad is through nuts, seeds, and oily fruits like avocado. In my Brazilian Heart of Palm Salad, the only oil comes from avocado diced in the salad. That being said, I think it is more important to focus on eating more greens and vegetables, and I think that is much easier to do, especially at first, if you use familiar, tasty dressings. My bottom line: Don't say no to dressings. Say yes to lots more greens and veggies.

To answer the other question "isn't low-fat dairy better" I can only say that if most of your diet is made up of dairy, low-fat might be better. But if most of your diet is made up of vegetables and fruits, then the dairy that is in your diet is probably there to add flavor, and in dairy products, the flavor is carried primarily by the fats. In Europe, people are not as caught up in the "low-fat" fad as we are in the United States, and I think their attitude toward food is in many ways a healthier attitude. If you are interested in this subject, I highly recommend the book *French Kids Eat Everything*, listed in my recommended reading list, page 209.

SECTION 6

Drinks and Sweet Treats

- MINÄ PIDÄN MUSTIKOISTA
- RECIPES
- FREQUENTLY ASKED QUESTIONS

MINÄ PIDÄN MUSTIKOISTA

I love languages, so when I'm visiting in a country, I usually try to learn some of the language, if it's not one I already know. It's a testament to the difficulty of learning Finnish that in being around my Finnish friend Susanna, and in visiting her family for several days, I only learned to count to six and learned to say one single phrase: *Minä pidän mustikoista*—I like blueberries. There was a good reason I learned that particular phrase. While I was visiting in Finland, Susanna's mother took me out gathering wild mushrooms and berries. I got to pick and eat wild blueberries off the bushes. They were probably the best berries I have ever had.

When I started trying to Eat Green, I sat down and thought about the fruits and vegetables I have loved. I thought about my experience with blueberries and that I really like fresh blueberries and that I never buy them. I knew blueberries were expensive, but, I thought, so are desserts, and if I ate fresh blueberries instead of dessert I would be just as happy; especially because of the fact they are a little bit of a splurge. It would make me feel like I was getting something really special.

The more I Eat Green, the more I think that when it comes to sweet treats, the very best kind are the ones that grew that way: a juicy mango, a perfectly ripe piece of watermelon, a cherry just off the tree in the early summer, a grape that has just the right combination of crunch and juiciness. In this section I have a some suggestions for fun ways to eat fruit as dessert and also a single, really good fruit smoothie recipe that can work with any single fruit or combination of two or three fruits.

While fruit is the healthiest dessert, I think that candies, cookies, and pies have their place too. I can't think of winter holidays without thinking of flavors like gingerbread, pumpkin pie, and mint chocolate. So I also have a series of treats I call "Bake-Me-Nots"—delicious cookie-dough-like bites that are quick to make, easy to store, and unforgettable! My bake-me-nots treat recipes and also my bake-me-not pumpkin pie recipe are based on ingredient combinations commonly used in the raw food movement. (Look up "raw vegan cookie recipes" online to find more recipes for this type of treat). The important

thing to keep in mind with these special goodies is that one shouldn't live on them. The Merriam-Webster Dictionary defines treat as "something that is pleasing to eat because it is rare or a luxury." I feel like the good things in life are there to be enjoyed and appreciated, but that the best way to do that is to Eat and Drink Green and to treat treats as treats!

brazilian limeade concentrate

I learned to make this from a family in Brazil. It has wonderful flavor and is so refreshing!

INGREDIENTS	1X
water	2 cups
limes	6 large
sugar	2½ cups

INSTRUCTIONS

1. Place the water in a blender. Wash and cut about a quarter to half inch off each end of each of the limes. Cut the limes in quarters.

2. Place two of the quarters in the blender. Pulse a couple of times. The pulp of the lime should look like it has been juiced but the peel should be mostly intact.

3. Pour the lime water through a strainer into a pitcher. Throw away the limes (assuming they look like as described in step 2. If they don't look like they have been juiced, try pulsing again in the blender).

4. Pour the lime water back into the blender and repeat steps two and three until you have used up all the limes. Strain out the last limes and return the juice to the pitcher of your blender.

5. Add the sugar and blend to combine.

6. To serve: Dilute one part concentrate with two parts water.

TIPS AND VARIATIONS

- You will need to experiment a little with the first batch to see how long you need to run the blender each time.
- This limeade doesn't have the sweetened condensed milk that some Brazilian limeades do but still has that same fresh, zippy flavor.
- I've tried making this with honey and agave, but nothing really works like sugar in this recipe.
- Another way to make this: Cut off the ends of the limes as described in step 1. Slice each lime into thin slices. Place the lime slices and the sugar in a 2-quart container with a lid. Shake the container until all the slices are coated with sugar. Let stand for 30–60 minutes or until the lime slices look like they have been juiced. Add 3 cups of water, put on the lid, and shake vigorously. Immediately strain out the lime peel. Add ice and dilute as desired.

great fruit smoothie

I love this fruit smoothie recipe because the amounts are easy to remember, you can use it with a lot of different fruits and fruit combinations, and it keeps well in the fridge. I also like it because it tastes great with just one or two fruits (it's not complicated), and it has a thick, creamy texture without using any dairy.

INGREDIENTS	1X	2X
Fruit juice or water	3–4 oz.	3–8 oz.
coconut oil	1½–2 Tbsp.	3–4 Tbsp.
fresh fruit or thawed frozen fruit	8 oz.	1 lb.
frozen fruit	8 oz.	1 lb.
Makes:	~2½ cups	~5 cups

INSTRUCTIONS

1. Measure the juice into your blender (sharp-blade or high-power). Add the coconut oil and fresh or thawed fruit. Blend until totally smooth and all one color. There should be no chunks of coconut oil and it should look creamy—like the texture of yogurt. Whether this takes a short time or a longer time will depend on your blender and the starting temperature of the ingredients.

2. Add the frozen fruit (you can use ice instead of about ⅓ of the fruit). Blend until smooth. Can be refrigerated for up to 24 hours or frozen to use later.

SUGGESTED COMBINATIONS

- *Apricot Sunrise*: orange juice, fresh apricots, frozen pineapple. This smoothie will keep its flavor and thick milk shake-like texture for 48 hours in the fridge because the orange juice and pineapple help preserve it.
- *Just Peachy*: orange juice, fresh or thawed peaches, frozen peaches. Can add four ounces frozen raspberries instead of four ounces of the frozen peaches in the 1x recipe. (Doesn't keep as well as Apricot sunrise. Drink or freeze right away)
- *Strawberry Nectarine*: white grape juice, fresh nectarines, frozen strawberries (or vice-versa).
- *Mango Lime*: limeade, fresh mango and frozen mango
- *Pineapple Treat*: cranberry juice, fresh strawberries, frozen pineapple.

TIPS

- Sweeter, more flavorful fruit equals better smoothie. Depending on your fruit and whether you use fruit juice you may need to sweeten your smoothie. I usually

use agave because it's so easy to mix in (even when the smoothie is all done), doesn't have to dissolve like sugar does, and has a relatively neutral flavor.

- For tips on measuring coconut oil, see page 203.
- The 2x recipe calls for less water or juice because you only need this liquid to get your blender started. You can add more or less of the juice/water depending on what your blender can handle and how thick you want the smoothie to be.
- If the smoothie gets a little bit warm during the first step, it doesn't matter—it will be cooled down again in the next step.
- The Apricot Sunrise smoothie is my favorite way to use apricots off of my tree in the summer. I make extra batches of smoothie and freeze it in empty disposable water bottles to pull out during the winter. For instructions on thawing the smoothies, see page 27.
- When peaches are at their best in the summer, I freeze them to use in smoothies. To freeze for smoothies: Wash the peaches in warm water to remove as much of fuzz as you can. Quarter the peaches, remove the pit, and freeze using one of the methods on page 14.
- I cut and freeze my own pineapple (see page 14), but you can get frozen pineapple at some grocery stores. I have also seen frozen mango in some stores.

Ways to Hydrate

One of the things I think is really great about eating lots of greens, is that, because of their high water content, it's a little easier to "stay hydrated." Most of us don't drink anywhere near the recommended amount in the first place, and even with the smoothies and salads, most people probably need more water. For many years I spent summers as the cook at a girls camp located at 8,500 feet. At that altitude, staying hydrated is really challenging and I became very aware of the need to eat plenty of fresh fruits and vegetables (a great source of electrolytes) and drink plenty of liquids. For some people though, its hard to drink water. They just don't like the taste. Drinking drinks with lots of sugar or artificial sweetener isn't healthy either and isn't as good for hydration. Over the years, I've collected a list of non-sweetened drinks and lightly sweetened drinks that can help you get the fluids you need.

- **Alkaline water**: There is a lot of hype and pseudoscience surrounding this water. Maybe it's healthier than regular tap water, maybe it's not—I'm not entirely convinced by the research that I've read. The bottom line with this water is that for me it tastes much better than regular or filtered water, so I will drink much more of it. I sometimes have problems drinking a lot of tap water on an empty stomach—it seems to give me sour stomach or make me feel hungry right away—but I don't have that problem at all with alkaline water. Because it's easier for me to get myself to drink it, I don't mind paying a little bit for it and going to the bother to keep it on hand.
- **Ginger infused water**: A friend in Germany introduced me to this great winter drink. She likes it because it doesn't need sweetening and is something she can sip all day. Here's how you make it: Cut off about ¼ ounce of fresh ginger root. Peel it and slice it and place it in an 8- to 10-ounce mug. Pour boiling water over it to fill the mug, and let it steep 2–3 minutes. Enjoy. Repeat. (You can use the same ginger several times without it losing its flavor.) *Note*: If you don't peel the ginger, it will float to the top of the water and give the infusion a bitter flavor.
- **Mint water**: My husband likes to take this to work to sip during the day. It is similar to the "MetroMint" water you can buy. Here's how you make it: To 20 ounces of water, add 4–5 drops of mint extract. Shake and enjoy. Avoid getting mint extract on the mouth of the bottle when you measure it because it can cause an unpleasant burning sensation if you get it on your lips. *Tip*: If you buy a new bottle of mint extract, leave the foil covering on the top and just cut a small slit in it with a knife—this makes it much easier to measure out a few drops.
- **Pomegranate water**: The flavor of this is subtle but tasty. I like it much better than many of the more well-known infused waters (like cucumber water); plus, if you make this in a clear glass pitcher of ice water, it looks very festive! Here's how you make it: Add a handful of pomegranate arils to your water. Crush the pomegranate seeds a little. Stir. Enjoy. Keep cold or use within a few hours.
- **Hot honey-orange-hibiscus infusion**: This tastes wonderful when you are coming down with a cold. Here's how you make it:

1. Heat three cups of water to boiling. Add three or four bags hibiscus or hibiscus/rose hip fruit "tea" (available in European, Middle Eastern, and some South American import stores. It contains only dried hibiscus flowers or dried hibiscus flowers plus rose hips).

2. Let steep five to eight minutes.

3. Remove "tea" bags. Stir in 1–2 heaping tablespoons of honey. When it is dissolved, add one cup of fresh squeezed orange juice. Makes one quart. Serve hot or chilled.

Note: If you have a hibiscus bush you can collect the petals of the flowers and dry them to use in this recipe.

- **Mint-cranberry chilled summer drink**: Some friends of ours served this wonderful drink when we visited them for a summer picnic. It was refreshing and delicious! It can be a good way to use your mint if you have it growing in your yard. Instructions from my friend:

1. Make about 8 cups of mint tea (I use the herb when it is taking over my lawn—you can also just use tea bags).

2. Put in ¼ cup honey. Stir to dissolve. Pour the mixture into a one-gallon container.

3. Add about two cups cold water or ice, and then fill to the top with Cran-Raspberry juice. Enjoy!

- **Fruit syrups**: European import stores (and Ikea) often carry concentrated fruit syrups for making juice drinks. Common flavors include black current, lingonberry and elderberry (flower or fruit.) These syrups do contain sugar, but they also have a lot of flavor and you can add as much or as little syrup to a glass of water as you want.

Fun with Fresh Fruit

There are so many fun ways to eat fresh fruit!

- **Apple sections dipped in sucanat**: Sucanat is a type of brown sugar—less refined than white sugar. It has excellent crunch and a pleasant caramel flavor. My nieces and nephews love dipping apple pieces in their own bowls of sucanat. They will choose this treat over candy when given the option. You can find sucanat in most grocery stores near the sugar.
- **Fresh blueberries**: I've already talked about eating berries as a treat, but I think it is worth repeating—berries are fun to eat and yummy!
- **Clementines**: When they are in season, clementine sections are like candy, and people can't get enough of them. (Trader Joe's dried Clementines, while not fresh, are also a fun way to enjoy some fruit).
- **Fruit skewers**: 6-inch skewers, threaded with fruit are hard to resist—for adults or kids. Do a variety of fruit pieces (melon, grapes, strawberries) or do just squares of watermelon for a refreshing summer treat.
- **Fruit with cream**: When the peaches come on in late summer, there is no better dessert than a really ripe peach, peeled and cut into small pieces with a little half-and-half poured over them.
- **Cherries on a straw**: Children sometimes have a hard time eating cherries because of the pits, but they can have a great time using a plastic drinking straw to remove the pits and then threading the cherries onto the straw.
- **The whole coconut**: Breaking open a real, ripe coconut is a fun activity. There's so much suspense in getting it open and seeing and tasting fresh coconut.
- **Grilled pineapple**: One word: Yum.
- **Bacon-wrapped Dates**: Most people think of dates as a dried fruit, but in fact, when you buy them whole in the store, they are almost always fresh—they just look dried. Bacon wrapped dates are easy to make. You just remove the pit (see Tip on page 200), put in a chunk of goat cheese *chevre* where the pit was, then wrap one-third of a piece of precooked bacon around the date, and secure it with a toothpick. Pan fry or grill until the bacon is crispy (or bake at 375 degrees for 10–12 minutes.) These taste great as an appetizer or alongside a green salad.
- **Broiled grapefruit**: In the winter, or when you want to feel "medieval," broiled grapefruit halves taste deliciously citrusy and spicy—like hot wassail. To make them, place grapefruit halves on a baking sheet. Poke the halves a few times with a knife so the toppings can flow down in and remove any seeds you find. Sprinkle halves with cinnamon and a little bit of ground cloves, then spread each half with ½–1 teaspoon brown sugar or sucanat. Place on an oven rack 4–6 inches under the broiler and broil on 400 degrees for 10 minutes.
- **Honeydew with lime**: Ripe honeydew melon tastes like a whole different melon if you drizzle it with fresh lime juice. If your melon isn't quite ripe, you can also sprinkle on a little powdered sugar.
- **Fresh nectarine**: Fresh ripe nectarines don't need anything to dress them up. Just cut them up and eat them. Delicious.
- **Fresh raspberries**: Nothing you can buy in the store can compare to berries picked in the patch. If you have never picked and eaten raspberries in the patch, put it on your calendar to go to a pick-your-own berry farm next June (or when berries are in season for you).

toasted coconut chips

These are a crispy, sweet treat that is easy to make and fun to have around.

INGREDIENTS	1X	2X
unsweetened flaked coconut	1 (7-oz.) bag	14 oz.
coconut oil	1 Tbsp. (½ oz.)	2 Tbsp. (1 oz.)
honey	3–4 Tbsp.	6–8 Tbsp.
salt	¼ tsp.	½ tsp.
baking pan	13 x 18 (half sheet)	2 (13 x 18) pans

INSTRUCTIONS

1. Gently heat the coconut oil and honey together until melted. Stir in the salt.
2. Pour over the coconut in a large bowl and toss together with the coconut until all the pieces are coated.
3. Spread evenly on a pan or pans lined with parchment.
4. Bake at 350 degrees for 8 minutes. Bake an additional 2–3 minutes while watching until desired toastiness is reached.

ranger cookie bake-me-nots

As the head cook at a girls camp, I would mix up a big batch of cookie dough, then scoop it into balls, and freeze it so we could bake the cookies fresh on the day we needed them. I allowed the staff to grab a ball of frozen cookie dough as a treat on their way past the kitchen when they didn't have campers with them. One particular cookie recipe was so popular as dough that I never ended up baking any of them and started making it specifically as a frozen treat. This recipe is based on that one, but is healthier.

INGREDIENTS	1X	2X
coconut oil	¼ cup (2 oz.)	½ cup (4 oz.)
real maple syrup	5–6 Tbsp. (3 oz.)	¾ cup (6 oz.)
vanilla extract	1 Tbsp.	2 Tbsp.
salt	¼ tsp.	½ tsp.
rolled instant oats	½ cup (1¾ oz.)	1 cup (3½ oz.)
unsweetened fine shred coconut	¾ cup (2¼ oz.)	1½ cups (4½ oz.)
almond flour	¾ cup (2¾ oz.)	1½ cups (5½ oz.)
cornflakes (optional)	½ cup (¾ oz.)	1 cup (1½ oz.)
Makes:	about 25 half-ounce treats	about 50 half-ounce treats

INSTRUCTIONS

1. Measure all the ingredients except the cornflakes into a mixing bowl or the bowl of a stand mixer.

2. Mix with an electric hand mixer or blade attachment of a stand mixer until the ingredients are well combined and resemble cookie dough.

3. Add the cornflakes and mix until combined.

4. Use a ½-ounce cookie scoop to scoop into small balls on a tray. Refrigerate. After they are cold, transfer them to a sealed container. Serve refrigerated or frozen.

TIPS

- This will keep for a few weeks in the refrigerator and several months frozen.
- This recipe is gluten free (as long as you use gluten free cornflakes and oats).

peppermint fudge bake-me-nots

These yummy chocolate-peppermint bites taste like fudgy mint cookie balls. They are relatively healthy and super-easy to make!

INGREDIENTS	1X	2X
maple syrup	2 oz. (¼ cup)	4 oz. (½ cup)
coconut oil	1 oz. (2 Tbsp.)	2 oz. (¼ cup)
cocoa powder	¼ cup	½ cup
vanilla	2 tsp.	4 tsp.
salt	a pinch	⅛ tsp.
unsweetened fine shred coconut	¾ cup (2½ oz.)	1½ cups (5 oz.)
almond flour	1 cup (3½ oz.)	2 cups (7 oz.)
crushed peppermint candy	2–4 Tbsp. (½–1¼ oz.)	¼–½ cup (1–2½ oz.)
Makes:	about 20 half-ounce treats	about 40 half-ounce treats

INSTRUCTIONS

1. Mix together the maple syrup, coconut oil, and cocoa powder. Mix until they are well combined and there are no lumps of coconut oil.

2. Add the salt and vanilla, and mix.

3. Add the finely shredded coconut, almond flour, and peppermint pieces, and mix until the mixture holds together like cookie dough.

4. Scoop with a very small (½-oz.) cookie scoop or roll into a log, cut in pieces, and roll each piece into a ball shape. Place formed cookies on a plate or tray.

5. Allow to dry overnight or for about 8 hours at room temperature in a cool, dry location. Store in a tightly sealed container.

TIPS AND VARIATIONS

- Two tablespoons crushed peppermint candy is equivalent to 4 round peppermint candies, crushed.
- I use "raw" cocoa in these cookies because I love the flavor. You can use any kind of baking cocoa, but may need to tweak the amounts. You can get raw cocoa online or at health food stores.
- Letting the cookies "dry" makes them so they won't stick to each other once they are put away.
- The cookies will keep their best flavor several weeks at room temperature, several months in the fridge, and at least a year if frozen.

speculoos bake-me-nots

If you have had Biscoff cookies on a airplane or cookie butter, you know the wonderful spicy flavor profile of the cookies these treats are based on. Called Spekulatius in Germany, Speculaas in the Netherlands, and Speculoos in Belgium—they are delicious wherever you eat them. This recipe captures the flavor of the cookies while being quick to make, flourless, and relatively nutritious!

INGREDIENTS	1X	2X
coconut oil	2 oz. (4 Tbsp.)	4 oz. (8 Tbsp.)
maple syrup	3 oz. (6 Tbsp.)	6 oz. (¾ cup)
molasses	1–1½ Tbsp.	2–3 Tbsp.
instant rolled oats	½ cup (1¾ oz.)	1 cup (3½ cups)
salt	⅛ tsp.	¼ tsp.
cinnamon	1 tsp.	2 tsp.
cloves	½ tsp.	1 tsp.
nutmeg	⅛ tsp.	¼ tsp.
ginger (powdered, dry)	⅛ tsp.	¼ tsp.
almond flour	1 cup (3½ oz.)	2 cups (7 oz.)
sliced almonds (optional)	½ cup (3½ oz.)	1 cup (7 oz.)
Makes:	about 20 half-ounce treats	about 40 half-ounce treats

INSTRUCTIONS

1. Mix the coconut oil, maple syrup, and molasses together using an electric hand mixer or stand mixer. Add the oats, salt, and spices, and mix to combine.

2. Add the almond flour and sliced almonds if using. Mix. If using sliced almonds, mix until they have been broken up into small pieces. Mixture should resemble cookie dough.

3. Scoop into balls with a small (½ oz.)cookie scoop. Allow to dry uncovered at room temperature for about 8 hours, then place in a sealed container for storage.

TIPS AND VARIATIONS

- Depending on room temperature in your house and time of the year, your coconut oil might be quite hard. If it is, you may want to heat the maple syrup before you add it so that it will soften the coconut oil as they mix.
- For best results, store bake-me-nots in tightly sealed container in fridge or freezer after they have dried. Can also be stored in tightly sealed container at room temperature for a few weeks.
- Try adding a little orange or lemon zest to the recipe for a fun flavor twist.

bake-me-not "pumpkin" pie

This pie ends up looking and tasting a lot like pumpkin pie but has ingredients more like you would find in a fruit salad. A Waldorf salad generally contains apples, raisins, nuts, and some kind of oil (mayo or cream). This "salad" has raw sweet potato, dates, nuts, and coconut oil. It takes a little more work than some of my recipes and must be made 48 hours in advance of when you want to serve it, but it is a fun way to eat something that is, in essence, a salad!

INGREDIENTS	½X	1X (9″ PIE)
water	4 oz. (½ cup)	8 oz. (1 cup)
coconut oil	1½ oz. (3 Tbsp.)	3 oz. (6 Tbsp.)
chia	2 tsp.	4 tsp.
dates, pits and stems removed	3 ½–4 oz. or about 7 dates	7–8 oz. or about 15 dates
cinnamon	1½ tsp.	3 tsp.
cloves	¼ tsp.	½ tsp.
nutmeg	a dash	⅛ tsp.
real maple syrup	½–1 Tbsp.	1–2 Tbsp.
sweet potato, peeled, raw	5 oz.	10 oz.
pecans	1 oz. or about ¼ cup	2 oz. or about ½ cup
almond flour	1½ oz. or about ½ cup	3 oz. or about 1 cup
Serves (as pudding or pie):	4–5	8–10

INSTRUCTIONS

1. Prepare your crust (recipe follows).

2. Measure water into blender. Add coconut oil, chia, dates, spices and maple syrup. Turn the blender on to a low or medium low speed until the dates are chopped. Scrape down the sides, then switch to the highest speed. Process until the mixture is completely smooth and all one color with a thick, creamy texture. Try a taste to make sure there are no chunks of date. It should taste a bit like gingerbread.

3. Peel a sweet potato and weigh out the amount you need. Cut into small pieces and process with the pecans in a food processor until finely chopped. Add this

mixture to the blender and process until smooth. Remove from blender stand and stir by hand to check for chunks. If there are still chunks of sweet potato, process until they are gone.

4. If you have a sharp-blade blender: transfer the mixture to a mixing bowl and mix in the almond flour. If you have a high-power blender: add the almond flour and blend until it is incorporated.

5. Pour the pie mixture into the crust. Refrigerate 48 hours before serving.

TIPS

- When it comes to food safety, I tend to be extra careful when I am making a salad. When food is cooked, germs are killed, but in salads, there's no cooking, so bacteria and especially viruses can be easily spread. In food service, the rule is "no bare-handed contact with ready-to-eat foods"; in other words, gloves or tongs should be used when handling foods that aren't going to be cooked before they are eaten. When I make this recipe, it reminds me so much of making a baked pumpkin pie that I have to keep reminding myself that I should treat it like a salad. This is especially important because this pie must be refrigerated for two days before serving. Pathogens multiply slowly at refrigerator temperature, but they can still multiply. I encourage you to follow the "no bare hand contact" rule when handling the sweet potato and the pie filling mix!
- Refrigerating the pie for two days allows the spices to blend and mellow. The moisture levels also equalize between ingredients creating a better texture. Tastes best 2–3 days after you make it.
- For those that follow the raw food movement, this pie qualifies as a raw, vegan food. It is also sugar-free, gluten-free, and egg-free (but not nut-free.) If you have someone with an almond allergy, you can substitute finely ground raw macadamia nuts for the almond flour in the pie and in the crust.
- If you end up with too much filling for your crust, put the extra filling in a bowl, refrigerate it, and eat it as "pumpkin pudding." If you don't want to make enough for a whole pie, make the ½x recipe and serve it as pudding.
- This is a nutritious recipe for kids (ones that are old enough to have nuts). My nephews (2 years and 4 years) gobble this up (even though they are still trying to decide if they like green smoothies).
- It's easy to take the pit out of dates. Just make a slit along one side of the date and pull the pit out—the pits are loose inside the date and come right out.

CRUST FOR BAKE-ME-NOT "PUMPKIN" PIE

INGREDIENTS	1X
almond flour	4 oz. (1 cup)
whole raw pecans	2 oz. (½ cup)
coconut oil	½–¾ ounce (1–1½ Tbsp.)
maple syrup	1 tsp.
salt	a pinch

INSTRUCTIONS

1. Get out a 9-inch pie tin or glassware pie-dish and "dust" it with a little cinnamon.

2. Place all the crust ingredients in a food processor in the order listed. Process until mixture resembles cookie dough. (When finished, the dough should look and taste something like shortbread cookie dough.) If you don't have a food processor, you can finely chop the pecans in some other way, and then combine all the ingredients with a mixer.

3. Press the dough evenly into the pie tin or dish to form a crust. Chill the crust in the refrigerator or freezer while you make the filling.

FREQUENTLY ASKED QUESTIONS

WHY DO YOU USE AGAVE IN YOUR RECIPES?

A few years ago, agave was the new "healthy" kind of sugar. Now research is showing it probably isn't any better than any other type of sugar. To understand this, you have to understand that in science, "sugar" doesn't just mean white table sugar like we use the word but refers to a whole class of related molecules that are used by the body in similar ways. The bottom line with any sugar—including sucrose, fructose, dextrose, and lactose—is that it isn't good for the body to have it straight, without any fiber or protein. Having lots of sugar straight has been linked to pre-diabetes and other health problems. Most of the agave I use in this book is in salad dressings. I prefer it over granulated sugar in that context because it dissolves and becomes part of the dressing so easily. I prefer it over honey or maple syrup in most situations because of its mild, almost neutral flavor.

In the context of a salad, we are talking about a little sugar with a lot of high-nutrient, high-fiber greens. This, to me, is a good use of sugar. My bake-me-not treats by contrast have quite a lot of "sugar" (usually maple syrup) in proportion to the amount of fiber and nutrients. That is why I emphasize that they are "treats"—something to eat occasionally and enjoy all the more because you don't have them all the time. As sweeteners go, honey, maple syrup, and agave do have more minerals than refined sugar, but the amount of nutrients per calorie from sugar is still very low, so that is why I think they should be used sparingly.

For my thoughts on artificial sweeteners, see Tip on page 146.

YOU RECOMMEND EATING FRUIT AS "DESSERT." DOES THIS MEAN YOU ARE SAYING FRUIT SHOULD BE EATEN ONLY OCCASIONALLY, LIKE SUGAR?

When my husband and I first started doing an "Eat, Drink, and Be Green" diet, we used fruit as a substitute for sugary treats. We would often eat some kind of fresh berry as an evening snack. We bought pre-cut watermelon to eat in the afternoon as a way to hydrate, get some nutrients, and have something sweet. The more we used fruit as a snack or dessert, the more we found that we didn't care as much about "normal" desserts like candy and cookies. After a few years of eating green, we still love fruit, but find that it's enough to have it in a smoothie and then only in a green salad or as an occasional dessert because it tastes sweeter to us than it used to. Some people say you can taste the more delicate flavors of food better when you aren't eating a lot of foods with a super-high proportion of sugar to other ingredients, and I think that is true.

When people with diabetes try to start eating green, they have to be careful about how much fruit they consume because fruit contains a lot of fructose, one of the types of sugar. This can make starting to eat green a little bit more of a delicate balance. It's one of the reasons I say that it is better and easier to start eating green while you are still healthy.

WHY DO YOU USE COCONUT OIL?

Raw coconut oil is composed mostly of medium-chain fatty acids, a type (or size) of molecule rarely found in other oils. Medium chain fatty acids may have several health benefits; the research is still being done, but looks promising. One thing that does seem to be certain is that medium-chain fatty acids don't affect cholesterol levels in the body—positively or negatively. Raw coconut oil has a pleasant, creamy flavor that works well in my fruit smoothie and my bake-me-not recipes. It has been a part of island diets for hundreds, if not thousands of years. This link has a list of peer-reviewed scientific articles relating to coconut oil: http://coconutoil.com/peer_reviewed/.

I FIND COCONUT OIL DIFFICULT TO MEASURE. DO YOU HAVE ANY SUGGESTIONS?

Coconut oil can be a pain to measure, unless you use a cookie scoop for the job (see page 5). I have two ½-ounce scoops, so I generally keep one of the scoops in an empty glass jar next to my coconut oil. That way I can use it whenever I need to measure coconut oil and don't have to wash it between each use. Even if I am using a scoop to portion it, I generally weigh the oil as I measure it. I place the bowl on the scale, zero the scale, and then add coconut oil until the scale reads the amount I needed for the recipe. If I am measuring raw coconut oil and get some on my skin, I just rub it in—it makes a high-quality lotion.

DO I NEED TO REFRIGERATE COCONUT OIL?

Not unless you want to. Coconut oil is very stable and will keep a long time without going rancid, even at room temperature.

Conclusion

If you are holding this book, there is a good chance that part of your brain is letting you know that there is something in this book you have been looking for.

In the book *Blink: the Power of Thinking Without Thinking,* Malcolm Gladwell uses research done in diverse fields to show that there is a type of thinking we do that occurs in the blink of an eye. This "instinctive thinking" is so fast that we don't recognize it as "thinking." He explains: "We live in a society dedicated to the idea that we're always better off gathering as much information and spending as much time as possible in deliberation. But I don't think this is true. There are lots of situations . . . when our snap judgments and first impressions offer a much better means of making sense of the world." (from http://gladwell.com/blink/blink-q-and-a-with-malcolm/). His conclusion? "Truly successful decision making relies on a balance between deliberate and instinctive thinking."

When I first picked up the book my friend had lent me about intensely green smoothies, I was skeptical, but at some point as I was reading, all the information I had been gathering for years seemed to "click" together with one new piece of information and in a "blink," I was convinced that intensely green smoothies were something I wanted to try, and, in fact, *needed* to try. Gladwell says, "The key to good decision making is not knowledge. It is understanding." One of the ways to get from "knowledge" to "understanding" is to take action. I have set my book up in a way to make it easy to take action: to do one thing from my "fridge list" (page 3); to try one green smoothie, and then, maybe, try another.

IF YOU TRY A GREEN smoothie, you might find you like it.
If you find you like it, you might start drinking green smoothies every day.
If you start drinking green smoothies every day, you might start craving greens.
If you start craving greens, you might start liking all kinds of vegetables too.
If you start liking all kinds of vegetables, you might find it easy and fun to Eat Green.
And if you find it easy and fun to Eat Green, you might start making green smoothies for others you know.
And if others you know try a green smoothie, they might find they like it.

(Done in the style of the well-loved book If You Give a Mouse a Cookie *by Laura Joffe Numeroff.)*

It's not easy to sort through all the available information and come to conclusions about how to take care of one's own health. But I think the only way to really know is to trust the thoughts that come in those "blink of an eye" moments—enough to take action and see where it gets you.

I wish you the best in your own steps to Eat, Drink, and Be Green!

—Michele Nielson

Acknowledgments

Every member of my family—my parents, siblings, brother-and sisters-in-law, nieces, and nephews and their spouses and kids—helped in a real way make this book happen and I couldn't have done it without them. It also simply wouldn't have happened without my husband's ability to help me weigh ideas but also make "blink" type decisions in critical moments.

My immediate neighbors and a few friends also offered support at critical times and made a difference. The inspiration for the title of this book came from my niece, Elyse Pehrson. Several people allowed me to use their recipes in this book and their names are on the various recipes.

LIST OF FAQS

Recommended Reading List

Gladwell, Malcolm. *Blink: The Power of Thinking Without Thinking*. Back Bay Books, 2007.

Campbell, Thomas and Campbell, T. Colin. *The China Study: The Most Comprehensive Study of Nutrition Ever Conducted And the Startling Implications for Diet, Weight Loss, And Long-term Health*. BenBella Books, 2006.

Le Billon, Karen. *French Kids Eat Everything: How Our Family Moved to France, Cured Picky Eating, Banned Snacking, and Discovered 10 Simple Rules for Raising Happy, Healthy Eaters*. William Morrow, 2012.

Food Matters Facebook page: https://www.facebook.com/foodmatters.

Physicians Committee for Responsible Medicine website: www.pcrm.org.

Boutenko, Victoria. *Green for Life: The Updated Classic on Green Smoothie Nutrition*. North Atlantic Books, 2010.

Fuhrman, Joel. *Eat to Live: The Amazing Nutrient-Rich Program for Fast and Sustained Weight Loss, Revised Edition*. Little, Brown and Company, 2011.

Openshaw, Robyn. *The Green Smoothies Diet: The Natural Program for Extraordinary Health*. Ulysses Press, 2009.

Index

D

E

F

G

H

I

J

K

R

S

T

U

V

W

Y

Z

About the Author

MICHELE NIELSON has had a lifelong interest in food preparation and loves testing and tweaking recipes. She spent many years as a kitchen manager at a girls camp where she was in charge of recipe development and also cooked daily for groups of two hundred. Her first book, *Dutch Oven Cookout: Step-by-Step* has been called "a Dutch Oven encyclopedia with its wealth of information in addition to recipes."

In *Eat, Drink, and Be Green,* Michele turns her hand to creating recipes that make high-nutrient meals easy and appealing. Her interest in food from other cultures has helped her come up with delicious combinations while her experience as a kitchen manager has honed her ability to keep recipes simple with easy-to-follow instructions.

Michele enjoys learning languages, taking photos of food, and re-creating recipes she has tasted in her extensive travels abroad. She enjoys eating healthy but is a foodie at heart. She believes food should taste good, especially when Eating Green!

Photo by Elyse Pehrson

This book has a special binding. It is similar to the binding you would normally find on a hard back book or textbook. With a little work, your binding will allow you to lay the book flat while you work from the recipes. To "break in" your binding, set the book on a flat surface with the spine against the work surface. Working from the front and back simultaneously, open a few pages at a time until you reach the center of the book. This should make the binding arch as shown in the photo. Repeat these steps until the book will lay open to the page you are working from.

0 26575 16140 3